Other books by Peggy Harrison and Jay Hosler:

Norm and Burny - The Black Square
Norm and Burny - The Girl With the Gold Coin
Rockslide
The Spirit Chamber
Ring of Fire

Recipes from Cinnamon Sticks Tea Room

A Collection of Recipes by
Paul and Peggy Harrison

Fifth Edition
Copyright 2016
Treehouse Enterprises
All rights reserved.
Reproduction in whole or in part
without written permission is prohibited.

ISBN-13: 978-0692743140
ISBN-10: 0692743146

Published by Treehouse Enterprises

DEDICATION

We would like to dedicate this book to all of the wonderful ladies who have worked with us through the years. Without their love, loyalty and hard work, Cinnamon Sticks would not have existed. We would also like to thank all of our faithful customers, many of whom have come to lunch in the Tea Room weekly for many years. We're grateful for your smiles, your compliments and your good wishes.

We miss all of you.

A BRIEF HISTORY OF CINNAMON STICKS

In 1985 an eight-person co-op was started at 124 South Main St. in Keller, Texas. The rooms were leased to different people, each with their own specialty. At the time, I was making primitive rag dolls, and was invited to sell them through one of the shops. A few months later, through an involved set of circumstances, Paul and I took over ownership of the co-op with two other couples, and Cinnamon Sticks was born. Through the years, as people left the co-op for whatever reason, we absorbed the space in lieu of releasing it.

In 1989 we started the Tea Room so that there would be a unique place for shoppers to have lunch. We initially used only one small room with four tables. By 1991 Paul and I were the sole owners of Cinnamon Sticks and the Tea Room had been expanded to part of the larger front room. The widening of Hwy 377, which runs in front of Cinnamon Sticks, took our fence and part of our front yard and prompted us to move the main entrance to the "back" of the shop; this gave us room to expand the Tea Room into the remaining front area. An upstairs room was eventually turned into dining space used mostly for private parties; that room was later moved downstairs where it is much easier to use.

As 2003 approached, we decided it was time to turn the Tea Room over to someone with fresh new ideas and do something else with our lives. We are now semi-retired...Paul keeps busy with his electronics work and I keep busy playing music, teaching and quilting. Since 2013 we are both also working on Wild Rose Heritage Center.

ABOUT THIS COOKBOOK

For a long time people have been asking us to do a cookbook of recipes we use in the Tea Room. Now that we are semi-retired we decided it was time to put the cookbook together. We hope you enjoy and use many of the recipes you will find here. Most are really quite simple and all are delicious. Paul and I have both contributed the recipes with which we are most familiar. Paul has always done the soups and many of the desserts as well as having developed most of the salads we use. My area has been desserts and afternoon teas, especially the elaborate teas we have done at Christmas and Mother's Day.

Along with the recipes, you will find personal notes we have written to make suggestions about the recipes or to give you a little idea about their history. Several have names and dates mentioned and we are indebted to the people who have shared wonderful recipes with us through the years. In addition to recipes from the Tea Room, I have included many that I use at home. Most of them are old, tried-and-true favorites that I have used for years. I hope you will find some that will become favorites for your family, too.

If you remember having something in our Tea Room that has not been included in the book, please let us know. We tried to remember as much as possible but we're sure we must have forgotten something. We will try to include those things in a future edition. If you would like to be informed via email of new additions or changes to this cookbook, send an email to:
cookbook@TreEnt.com

We use low salt ingredients whenever possible and a salt substitute (We use Mrs. dash, but there are others). For canned vegetables, we use the no-salt-added varieties when available. Otherwise, we drain and rinse to remove as much salt as possible. Salt may be added to taste, but start with the recipes as presented.

Chopped, cooked, white meat chicken is available in the frozen food section of most supermarkets, but you can cook your own, cool and chop it for lower cost.

When milk is called for, we use 1/2% milk. (Skim will usually work just as well). If you want a richer soup, use whole milk or half and half. Hey, go for it!

We use a commercial broth that we highly recommend: Minor's Low Sodium Chicken Broth is an excellent product that is available online (www.soupbase.com). They have many other concentrated broths - all are good. You can find other soup concentrates in the super market, but their salt content is so high that it is difficult to make a good broth with them.

Recipes we have used in the Tea Room have a teacup ( ) next to them.

For the most part, we have only one recipe per page We have added notes about some of the recipes and also inserted note pages for you to add your own.

Paul and Peggy Harrison

NOTES ON THE FIFTH EDITION

We keep trying new recipes and have decided to add a few of our favorites to this 2016 edition of our cookbook.

This is our first published edition. We hope you like it.

Enjoy!!

APPETIZERS & DIPS

APPETIZERS & DIPS

SPICY DIP

1 large carton cottage cheese (small curd)
1 (8 oz.) pkg. cream cheese, softened
1 jar jalapeno cheese whiz
1 pkg. ranch dressing mix
Hot sauce to taste (optional)

Blend ingredients in food processor until smooth. Put into serving bowl and chill to thicken. Good with raw vegetables, chips or crackers.

Yield: 2 1/2 cups

FIRE AND ICE

2 cups watermelon, drained and finely chopped
1 jalapeno pepper, seeded and diced
1 Tbsp. lime juice, fresh squeezed
1 Tbsp. cilantro, chopped
1 Tbsp. onion, diced

Mix ingredients together and marinate for about 4 hours. Drain well before serving. Good with chips or crackers.

Yield: 1-1/2 cups

APPETIZERS & DIPS

VEGETABLE BARS

Preheat oven to 350 degrees

2 (8 oz.) refrigerated crescent rolls
2 (8 oz.) pkg. cream cheese, softened
3/4 cup mayonnaise
1 envelope ranch dressing mix
3/4 cup each of:
Red bell pepper, finely chopped
Green onions, finely chopped
Broccoli, finely chopped
Carrots, finely chopped
Mushrooms, finely chopped
1 cup Cheddar cheese, grated (optional)

Cover bottom of 11x17 ungreased baking pan with crescent rolls by rolling out flat and pinching edges together to make a solid crust. Bake at 350 degrees for 7-8 minutes (not quite done). Cool.

Blend together cream cheese, mayonnaise and ranch dressing mix. Spread over cooled crust. Sprinkle each chopped, raw vegetable over top in an even distribution. Sprinkle with Cheddar cheese if desired. Use plastic wrap to cover top and push vegetables down into the cream cheese mixture. Chill 3-4 hours

NOTES:

Cut into smaller bars for appetizer or larger squares for a luncheon entree

APPETIZERS&DIPS

CREAM CHEESE TOASTED HORS'DOUVERS

2 (8oz.) pkgs. cream cheese, softened
1 cup Parmesan cheese
6 Tbsp. mayonnaise
8 green onions, finely chopped
1 loaf of bread, thin sliced, crusts removed

Mix together cream cheese, Parmesan cheese, mayonnaise and green onions. Toast slices of bread, on one side only, under the broiler. Cut into fourths. Spread cheese mixture thickly on UNTOASTED side of bread. Spread out on large cookie sheet and place in the freezer for about 1 hour. Put into freezer bag and store in freezer until ready to use.

To serve: Preheat broiler to 500 degrees. Place desired number of frozen pieces on a cookie sheet under broiler until mixture bubbles.

Makes about 100 squares.

NOTE: Watch the bread very carefully when you put it under the broiler to toast...it will burn quickly. With some breads, it is easier to cut the crusts off after toasting.

These are even delicious at room temperature, but they are especially yummy just out of the oven. This is a great make-ahead recipe and everyone loves them.

APPETIZERS&DIPS

SHORTBREAD CHEESE BALLS

Preheat oven to 350 degrees

1/2 lb. (2 sticks) unsalted butter, softened
2-1/2 cups flour, sifted
2 cups sharp Cheddar cheese, grated
1 cup pecans or walnuts, chopped
2 tsp. salt
1/2 tsp. cayenne pepper or to taste

Mix all ingredients well; mixture will appear loose and dry. Place about ¼ cup into the palm of your hand and squeeze into a ball (I transfer the mixture from hand to hand as I shape it). Form into 3/4" balls. Place on ungreased baking sheet and flatten slightly with the tines of a fork. Bake at 350 degrees for 15 minutes. Transfer to paper towels to cool.

Makes about 3-4 dozen depending on how big you make the balls.

 NOTES:

These make wonderful appetizers. The fact that it is a savory shortbread always surprises people.

APPETIZERS & DIPS

SPINACH POPPERS

Preheat oven to 350 degrees

1 small can artichoke hearts, drained and chopped
1-15 oz. pkg. chopped frozen spinach, thawed and drained
1-10 oz. carton (1 cup) part-skim ricotta cheese
2 eggs, beaten
1 clove garlic, minced
1/4 cup red onion, minced
1/2 tsp. fresh oregano, minced
1/4 cup shredded part-skim mozzarella cheese
Fresh ground pepper and salt to taste

Mix all ingredients together in a large bowl. Spray mini-muffin tins with cooking spray and fill with popper batter. Bake 25-30 minutes, remove from oven and serve warm.

Makes 18

APPETIZERS&DIPS

PIMENTO CHEESE

1 (3oz) pkg. cream cheese, softened
1 cup grated sharp Cheddar cheese
1 cup grated Monterey Jack cheese
1/2 cup mayonnaise or plain yogurt
3 Tbsp. pimentos, minced
1 tsp. onion, grated (optional)
1/4 cup chopped green chilies
Generous amount of fresh ground black pepper

Beat cream cheese with electric mixer until fluffy. Add remaining ingredients and beat until well blended.

Serve with chips or crackers.

Yield: 3 cups

Notes:

APPETIZERS & DIPS

CRANBERRY-CHILI CHEESE SPREAD

1 (8 oz) package cream cheese, softened
1 can (14 oz) whole-berry cranberry sauce
1 can (4 oz) green chilies, finely sliced
1 Tbsp. lime juice
1/2 tsp. garlic powder
1/2 tsp. cayenne pepper
1/2 tsp. chili powder

Place cream cheese on a serving place. In a small bowl, combine the cranberry sauce, green chilies, onion, lime juice and spices. Spoon over cream cheese. Serve with crackers.

Yield: 2 cups

APPETIZERS & DIPS

SPICY CRANBERRY SALSA

1 (8 oz) package cream cheese, softened
1/2 cup granulated sugar
1/2 cup packed light brown sugar
1 cup water
1 (12 oz) pkg. fresh or frozen cranberries
1-3 Tbsp. prepared horseradish (to taste)
1 Tbsp. Dijon mustard

In a large saucepan, bring white and brown sugars and water to a boil over medium heat. Stir in cranberries; return to a boil. Cook for 10 minutes or until thickened, stirring occasionally. Cool.

Stir in horseradish and mustard. Transfer to large bowl; refrigerate until chilled. Just before serving, spread cream cheese over crackers; top with cranberry salsa.

Yield: 2 1/2 cups

APPETIZERS&DIPS

SPICED SHRIMP COCKTAIL

1/2 cup cider vinegar or beer
1/2 cup water
2 Tbsp. Old Bay Seasoning
1 lb. large shrimp, peeled and deveined, leaving tails on
1 cup red seafood cocktail sauce

Mix vinegar, water and Old Bay Seasoning in medium saucepan. Bring to boil on medium heat. Gently stir in shrimp; cover.

Steam 2-3 minutes or just until shrimp turn pink. Drain well.

Serve immediately or refrigerate until ready to use. Serve with cocktail sauce.

Serves about 8

APPETIZERS&DIPS

SHRIMP AND AVOCADO BITES

1 avocado, peeled, seeded and chopped
1/2 lb. cooked, shelled shrimp, chopped
2 Tbsp. fresh chives, finely sliced
1 Tbsp. fresh basil, finely chopped
Juice of 1 lime
Salt and freshly ground pepper to taste

In a bowl, combine the avocado, shrimp, herbs and lime juice. Season with salt and pepper. Scoop the mixture onto crackers and serve.

Makes about 20

APPETIZERS & DIPS

BACON-WRAPPED WATER CHESTNUTS

Preheat oven to 350 degrees

2 cans whole water chestnuts
12 oz. bacon
1/2 cup dark brown sugar
1/4 cup chili sauce
1/4 cup mayonnaise

Wrap drained chestnuts in 1/3 piece of bacon and fasten with toothpick. Place on large foil-lined cookie sheet with 1" raised edges. Mix brown sugar, chili sauce and mayonnaise. Pour over chestnuts and bake for one hour or until bacon is crisp.

Makes about 2 dozen

APPETIZERS & DIPS

CHEDDAR-VEGETABLE TORTE

Preheat oven to 375 degrees

1-1/3 cups multigrain crackers, finely crushed
1/4 cup butter, melted
2 cups shredded sharp Cheddar cheese
1 small zucchini, finely chopped
5 small fresh mushrooms, sliced
1/3 cup red onion, finely chopped
1/4 cup sweet red pepper, finely chopped
1 Tbsp. olive oil
1 (8 oz) carton spreadable garlic and herb cream cheese
4 eggs, lightly beaten
2 Tbsp. bacon, cooked and crumbled
2 Tbsp. Parmesan cheese, grated

In a small bowl, combine cracker crumbs and butter; press onto the bottom of a greased 9" springform pan. Sprinkle with Cheddar cheese, In a large skillet, sauté the zucchini, mushrooms, onion and red pepper in oil until tender. Drain and spoon over cheese.

In a large bowl, beat herbed cream cheese until smooth. Add eggs; beat on low speed just until combined. Stir in cooked bacon. Pour over vegetable mixture. Sprinkle with Parmesan cheese.

Place pan on a baking sheet. Bake for 30-35 min. or until center is almost set. Cool on wire rack for 10 min. Carefully run a knife around edge of pan to loosen: remove sides of pan. Serve warm or chilled.

Yield: 16 servings

APPETIZERS & DIPS

CREAM CHEESE ROLLUPS

7 large (12") flavored tortillas
3 (8 oz.) Pkgs. cream cheese, softened
1/4 cup green chilies, chopped
1/4 cup pimentos, chopped
1/4 cup black olives, chopped
2 Tbsp. lemon juice, fresh squeezed

Mix together cream cheese, chilies, pimentos, olives and lemon juice. Add a little more lemon juice, if needed, to make mixture spreadable. Divide mixture equally among the seven tortillas. Spread evenly over tortillas to within about 1/2" of the edges.

Roll each tortilla from one edge, keeping as tight as possible all the way across. Wrap finished rolls individually in plastic wrap and refrigerate. When ready to serve, unwrap roll and slice to desired size, discarding end pieces. (In the Tea Room they usually got "discarded" into us!)

Variation: Cream cheese, lemon juice, chopped ripe olives and walnuts or pecans, chopped.

We used these for teas frequently and there was always one on our tea plate. All of us swear that Cinnamon Sticks was glued together with cream cheese!

We have tried herb tortillas and sun-dried tomato tortillas but we like the spinach tortillas the best.

APPETIZERS&DIPS

MEXICAN CORN DIP
Trisha Faubion, 2010

1 can white corn, drained
1 can Mexican corn, drained
1 small can chopped green chilies, drained
1 cup sour cream
1 cup mayonnaise
8 oz. cheddar cheese, grated
4 oz. pepper jack cheese, grated
1 cup green onions, chopped

Mix all ingredients together.   Chill before serving with chips, crackers or raw veggies.

Notes:

APPETIZERS&DIPS

MUHAMMARRA (ROASTED RED PEPPER AND WALNUT SPREAD)

This is a Middle-Eastern recipe and uses a specialty product: pomegranate molasses. I found it with the juices at Central Market. I've made it both with and without the pomegranate molasses and it really is best with.

2 red bell peppers, roasted and peeled (or the equivalent amount of roasted peppers in a jar)
2 slices rustic bread, torn into pieces
2 garlic cloves
1/2 cup walnuts, toasted
1 tsp. paprika
1/4 tsp. cayenne pepper
1 tsp. ground cumin
1 Tbsp. pomegranate molasses
1 Tbsp. extra-virgin olive oil
Juice of 1 lemon
 1/2 tsp. salt

Place peppers, bread, garlic and walnuts in a food processor and process for about 1 minute, scraping down sides once. Add the remaining ingredients and process until completely smooth, another minute or two. Taste and season with additional salt and lemon juice if needed.

Makes about 2 cups.

Good served with pita chips.

APPETIZERS & DIPS

SHRIMP DIP

1 -10 oz. can cream of shrimp soup
20 oz. cream cheese
1 -20 oz. package of precooked frozen baby shrimp, thawed
1/4 tsp. garlic salt

Mix softened cream cheese with soup. Pat excess water from thawed shrimp and chop into small pieces. Add to cream cheese mixture and stir in garlic salt. Chill before serving with chips or crackers.

Note:

If you can't find cream of shrimp soup, cream of mushroom works just as well. Low-fat cream cheese is fine to use. Add some fresh chives for color.

APPETIZERS & DIPS

GARDEN SALSA

6 medium tomatoes, finely chopped
3/4 cup green pepper, finely chopped
1/2 cup onion, finely chopped
1/2 cup green onions, thinly sliced
6 cloves garlic
1 tsp. cider vinegar
2 tsp. fresh lemon juice
2 tsp. olive oil
1-2 tsp. jalapeno pepper
1-2 tsp. ground cumin
1/2 tsp. salt
1/4-1/2 tsp. cayenne pepper

In a large bowl, combine all ingredients. Cover and chill until serving.

Makes about 5 cups. Serve with tortilla chips.

APPETIZERS & DIPS

SMOKY CHICKEN SPREAD

3 cups cooked chicken, finely chopped
1/2 cup celery, finely chopped
1/2 cup smoked almonds, coarsely chopped
3/4 cup mayonnaise
1/4 cup onion, finely chopped
1 Tbsp. honey
1/2 tsp. seasoned salt
1/8 tsp. black pepper

In a large bowl, combine all ingredients. Cover and chill at least 2 hours.

Makes about 4 cups. Serve with crackers or chips.

APPETIZERS&DIPS

BRUSCHETTA

Preheat oven to 350 degrees

1 French baguette, sliced about 1/4 " thick
2 roasted red peppers, chopped
4 Tbsp. parmesan cheese, grated
2 Tbsp. olive oil
1 clove garlic, minced
Seasoning salt, about 1/8 tsp.
2 Tbsp. balsamic vinegar
1 tsp. basil
1/8 tsp. oregano
1 Tbsp. green onion, chopped fine
Mozzarella cheese

Combine roasted red peppers, parmesan cheese, olive oil, minced garlic, seasoning salt, balsamic vinegar, basil, oregano and green onion. Gently warm sliced pieces of baguette for approximately 3 minutes. Remove baguette from oven and place prepared mixture on slices. Top with shredded mozzarella cheese. Return to oven on large cookie sheet for about 5 minutes until warm and mozzarella cheese has melted.

Note: line the cookie sheet with foil to catch drips. You can use either dried or fresh herbs.

APPETIZERS&DIPS

PHYLLO WRAPPED ASPARAGUS

(This is really a crossover recipe. It's good as an appetizer or as a side dish)

Preheat oven to 375 degrees

1 lb. fresh asparagus, tough ends chopped off
1/2 (16 oz.) package frozen phyllo dough sheets, thawed
1/4 cup butter, melted
1/4 cup Parmesan cheese, finely grated

Unwrap the phyllo sheets and cut the stack in half lengthwise. Reserve 1 stack for later use. Cover the phyllo with a slightly damp tea towel to keep it from drying out. Take 1 sheet of phyllo and brush lightly with some melted butter. Sprinkle with some Parmesan cheese. Place 2-3 asparagus spears (depending on size) on the short end of the sheet. Roll up, jelly-roll style. Place each piece, seam side down, on a baking sheet. Brush with more melted butter and sprinkle with more Parmesan. Repeat until all the asparagus spears are wrapped. Place baking sheet in oven and bake for 15-18 minutes or until golden brown and crispy.

Notes:

APPETIZERS & DIPS

SALADS

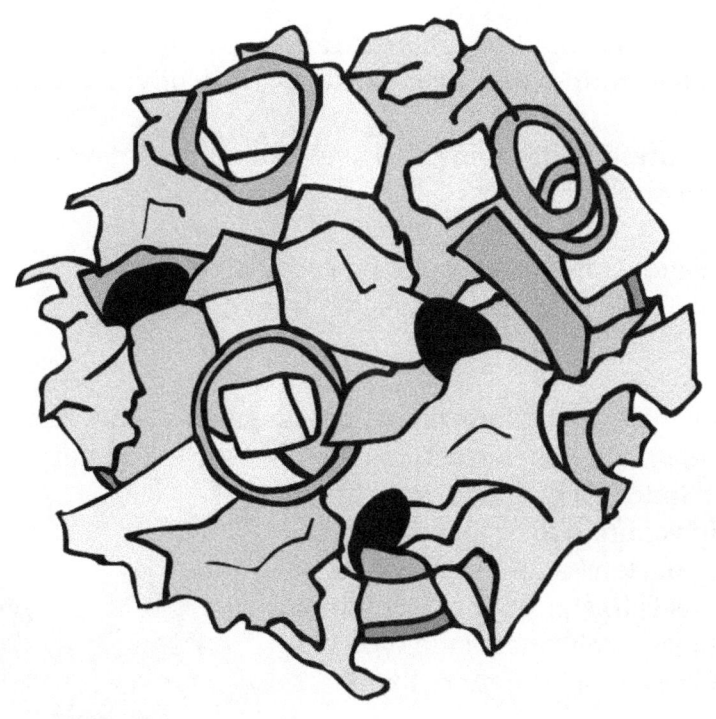

SALADS

CHICKEN SALAD

2 lb. cooked white meat chicken, cut into bite-size pieces
2 heads of celery, chopped
1 can ripe olives, diced

Marinade:
Juice of one lemon
1/4 tsp. cumin
1/2 tsp. dried dill
1/2 tsp. pepper
1 whole pimiento, chopped

Combine marinade ingredients and allow to rest for 10 minutes. Pour evenly over chicken, stir in olives and celery.

If you prefer a dressed salad, we recommend mayonnaise or ranch.

For sandwiches, chop in food processor to desired consistency, add mayonnaise to bind together.

NOTES:
Chicken salad was our most popular salad by far. It is based on Paul's recollection of a salad served at a diner in Fort Smith, Arkansas. The original recipe contained onions and mixed light/dark meat. An easy way to add onions is to stir 1/4 cup dehydrated onions into the marinade (you may need to add a little more lemon juice).

SALADS

SMOKED TURKEY SALAD

2 lb. of smoked turkey ham (Jennie-O is a good brand)
1/2 cup mayo
2 lemons
1 Tbsp. black pepper
1 Tbsp. dried dill
1/4 cup dehydrated onions

Juice the 2 lemons and add the pepper, dill and dehydrated onions. Let sit until all the lemon juice is absorbed

Chop the smoked turkey ham in a food processor. Add marinade and mayo and process to desired consistency - should be very fine.

NOTES:

People either love this recipe or don't care for it at all. If you like ham salad, you'll probably like this recipe. If you prefer to use ham instead of the smoked turkey, that will also work.

SALADS

CURRIED CHICKEN SALAD

1 lb. white meat chicken, cut into bite size pieces
1 cup grapes, cut in half
1 large can mandarin oranges (well drained)
1 cup mayonnaise
1 tsp. curry powder (or to taste)

Mix the curry powder and Mayo. Stir in all other ingredients. Serve on a lettuce leaf.

NOTES:

This is a relatively recent addition to our menu, and is an easy one to make. A mix of green and red grapes makes this an attractive salad.

Notes:

SALADS

SEAFOOD SALAD

1/2 lb. cooked, deveined salad shrimp
1/2 lb. Krab meat (artificial crab meat - you can use the real thing if you prefer)
1 cup celery, diced
1 lemon
2 tsp. dried dill
1 tsp. black pepper
1/4 cup dehydrated onions

To the juice of the lemon add the dill, pepper and dehydrated onions. Let sit until all the lemon juice is absorbed. Add the other ingredients and stir together.

Notes:

SALADS

TUNA SALAD

2 large cans tuna, drained
2 hard-boiled eggs, chopped
1 Tbsp. sweet pickle relish
1 Tbsp. dill pickle relish
1 Tbsp. mustard
2 Tbsp. red onion, finely chopped
1 Tbsp. sour cream
1/2 tsp. lemon pepper
1 tsp. dried dill
1/4 cup mayo

Combine all ingredients except for the tuna and eggs. Stir together well and add tuna and eggs.

Notes:

This is a variation on a recipe known as 'World's Best Tuna Salad'. You can find many other variations by searching the web. I like it made without the sweet pickle relish.

SALADS

BROCCOLI SALAD

2 lb. broccoli
10 slices bacon, cooked, drained and crumbled
4 green onions, chopped
1/2 cup raisins or dried cranberries
1/2 cup sunflower seeds (optional)
1 cup mayonnaise
1/4 cup sugar
2 Tbsp. cider vinegar

Remove leaves and tough stalks from broccoli, wash thoroughly and cut into small pieces. Place broccoli in a large bowl; add bacon, onion and raisins. Toss well. Combine mayonnaise, sugar and vinegar; whisk until smooth. Spoon dressing over salad and gently toss. Refrigerate at least 2-3 hours to allow flavors to blend. Letting it blend overnight is even better.

NOTES:

This is one of those salads people will ask you to bring to a potluck gathering time after time.

SALADS

GRAPE SALAD

2 lbs. green grapes, stemmed
2 lbs. red seedless grapes, stemmed
8 oz. sour cream
8 oz. cream cheese
1/2 cup granulated sugar
1 tsp. vanilla extract

Topping:
1 cup brown sugar, packed
1 cup toasted pecans, finely chopped

Wash, stem and dry grapes. Place in large mixing bowl. Mix sour cream, cream cheese, granulated sugar and vanilla by hand until blended. Pour mixture over the grapes, and stir to thoroughly coat. Pour into large serving bowl.

Combine brown sugar and nuts. Sprinkle over top of grapes to cover completely.

This works well as a salad or as a dessert. It's sweet and really yummy!

Chill overnight. Makes a ton!

SALADS

PINA COLADA FRUIT SALAD

1-1/2 cups green grapes, stemmed
1-1/2 cups seedless red grapes, stemmed
1-1/2 cups blueberries
1-1/2 cups fresh strawberries, halved
1 can (8 oz.) pineapple chunks, drained (or 1-1/2 cups of fresh pineapple cut into cubes)
1/2 cup fresh raspberries

1 can (10 oz.) frozen non-alcoholic pina colada mix thawed
1/2 cup sugar
1/2 cup pineapple-orange or straight orange juice
1/8 tsp. almond extract
1/8 tsp. coconut extract

In a large serving bowl, combine the first six ingredients. In a small mixing bowl, whisk the pina colada mix, sugar, juice and extracts until sugar is dissolved. Pour over fruit; toss to coat. Chill until ready to serve.

Makes about 8-10 servings

SALADS

BLACK BEAN SALAD

3 (15 oz.) cans black beans, drained and rinsed
2 cups corn, cooked fresh, frozen or canned (drained and rinsed)
1 green bell pepper, seeded and finely chopped
1 medium red onion, finely chopped
1/2 cup olive oil
1/4 cup red wine vinegar
1/4 cup fresh parsley, chopped
1/4 cup fresh cilantro, chopped
Salt and pepper (freshly ground) to taste

Combine all ingredients and mix thoroughly. Refrigerate, covered, for up to 2 days. If making in advance, add the parsley and cilantro immediately prior to serving.

Best served at room temperature. Makes 6-8 servings.

Notes:

SALADS

CRANBERRY MOLD

1 small pkg. raspberry jello
1 scant cup boiling water
1 can whole cranberry sauce
1 cup sour cream
1/2 cup celery, chopped (optional)
1/2 cup nuts, chopped (optional)

Dissolve raspberry jello in boiling water. Add cranberry sauce, sour cream, celery and nuts. Mix well and pour entire mixture into a 7" mold. Refrigerate overnight.

NOTES:

I don't know about you, but I've never had much luck "unmolding". Most of the time it either won't come out at all or it falls apart. Usually I just make this in a pretty serving bowl and let people scoop it out with a big spoon. My motto is: Easy is better.

SALADS

HAM SALAD

1 cup ham, diced
3 Tbsp. pimento, diced
2 Tbsp. green pepper, diced
1/2 cup onion, diced
1 egg, hard boiled, chopped
1 (8 oz.) can Chinese noodles

Combine ham, pimento, green pepper, onion and hardboiled egg in serving bowl.

Dressing:
3 Tbsp. mayonnaise
1 tsp. balsamic vinegar
1 tsp. milk
Dash of garlic powder

Blend together dressing ingredients. Chill. Add Chinese noodles and dressing just before serving. Makes a wonderful summer salad.

NOTES:

Try substituting bay shrimp for the ham.

SALADS

ROASTED SWEET POTATO SALAD WITH RED PEPPER VINAIGRETTE

Preheat oven to 400 degrees

4 large sweet potatoes, peeled and cut into bite-size pieces
1/2 cup olive oil, divided
Salt and freshly ground black pepper to taste
1/4 cup red-wine vinegar or sherry vinegar
1 medium red bell pepper, cored, seeded and quartered
2 tsp. ground cumin
1 Tbsp. grated orange zest
1/2 cup scallion, sliced or chopped green onions
1/2 cup fresh mint or parsley leaves, minced
1 or 2 fresh jalapenos or serranos, minced
1/4 cup raisins (optional)

Place sweet potatoes on a foil lined baking sheet, drizzle with 2 Tbsp. olive oil and toss to coat. Sprinkle with salt and pepper. Roast, turning occasionally, until crisp and brown outside and just tender inside. About 30 minutes. Set aside to cool.

While the potatoes are roasting, make the dressing. Pour the remaining 6 Tbsp. of oil into a blender along with the vinegar, bell pepper, cumin and zest. Sprinkle with a little salt and pepper. Puree until smooth. Toss the warm potatoes with the scallion (or green onions), mint or parsley, chilies and raisins (if using). Add 1/2 cup of the dressing and toss to coat. Add more dressing if you like and reserve the rest for people to add if they like.

Serve immediately or at room temperature. serves 6-8

SALADS

CRANBERRY WALDORF SALAD

1-1/2 cups fresh cranberries, chopped
1 cup red apple. chopped
1 cup celery, chopped
1 cup seedless green grapes, halved
1/3 cup raisins
1/4 cup walnuts, chopped
2 Tbsp. sugar
1/4 tsp. ground cinnamon
1 (8 oz) carton low-fat vanilla yogurt

Combine all ingredients and toss to coat. Cover and chill for about 2 hours. Stir just before serving. Makes 8-10 servings.

Notes:

SALADS

FRITO CORN SALAD

2 cans yellow whole kernel corn, drained
1/2 red bell pepper, chopped
1/2 green bell pepper, chopped
1/2 red onion, chopped
3/4 cup mayonnaise
1/4 cup horseradish
1 cup shredded Cheddar cheese
1 (5 oz.) bag of chili cheese flavor Frito corn chips

Mix all the ingredients except the chips. Add the chips in just before serving so they won't get soggy.

Serves about 12

SALADS

CRUNCHY NOODLE SALAD

1 (12 oz) coleslaw mix
2 (3 oz) packages instant ramen noodles (discard spice)
1 bunch green onions, chopped
4 oz. sesame seeds, toasted
4 oz. slivered almonds, toasted
1 tsp. ground ginger
1 tsp. ground pepper
1 tsp. garlic powder
1 tsp. onion powder
1/2 cup vegetable oil or sesame oil (NOT olive oil)
1/3 cup white wine vinegar or cider vinegar
1/4 cup sugar or Splenda

NOTE: Toast seeds and nuts FIRST. Ramen noodles may be toasted along with them to enhance the flavor. You can use the microwave: spread seeds, nuts, etc. out on a pan and watch carefully; 1 minute or less. Allow to cool.

Mix cabbage, sesame seeds and almonds together in large bowl. In a jar with a lid, mix the spices, oil, vinegar, sugar and green onions. Shake until well blended. Refrigerate separately.

When ready to serve: break raw ramen noodles into small pieces and blend into coleslaw mixture. Pour dressing over coleslaw and noodles and mix well.

SALADS

SUMMER CUCUMBER SALAD

1 medium cucumber, quartered and sliced
1 medium tomato, chopped
1/2 cup green pepper, chopped
1/3 cup sweet onion, chopped
2 Tbsp. fresh lime juice
2 Tbsp. red wine vinegar
3/4 tsp. dill weed
1/2 tsp. salt
1/4 tsp. pepper

In a large bowl, combine the cucumber, tomato, green pepper and onion. In a jar with a tight-fitting lid, combine lime juice, vinegar, dill, salt and pepper; shake well. Pour over cucumber mixture; toss to coat. Cover and refrigerate for 15 minutes. Serve with a slotted spoon.

Yield: 4 servings

SALADS

WHITE BEAN & TUNA SALAD

1 (19 oz.) can cannellini beans
1 (6 oz.) can white tuna packed in water
2 Tbsp. green onions, sliced
2 Tbsp. olive oil
1 Tbsp. balsamic vinegar
1 clove garlic
1 (4 oz.) can green chilies

Rinse and drain beans. Drain and flake tuna. Combine all ingredients. Refrigerate.

Serve with pita bread or pita chips or on a bed of lettuce.

Yield: 4 servings

SALADS

BALSAMIC GREEN BEAN SALAD

2 lbs. fresh green beans, trimmed and cut into pieces
1/4 cup olive oil
3 Tbsp. lemon juice
3 Tbsp. balsamic vinegar
1/4 tsp. salt
1/4 tsp. garlic powder
1/4 tsp. ground mustard
1/8 tsp. black pepper
1 large red onion, chopped
4 cups cherry tomatoes, halved
1 cup (4 oz.) crumbled feta cheese

Place beans in a Dutch oven and cover with water. Bring to a boil. Cover and cook for 8-10 minutes or until crisp-tender. Drain and immediately place beans in ice water. Drain and pat dry.

In a small bowl, whisk the oil, lemon juice, vinegar, salt, garlic powder, mustard and pepper. Drizzle over beans. Add the onion; toss to coat. Cover and refrigerate for at least 1 hour. Just before serving, stir in tomatoes and cheese.

Yield: 16 servings.

SALADS

SOUPS

SOUPS

NOTE:

We prepare our soups in a 6 quart slow cooker (a Presto). It is convenient, of sufficient heat output to be quick and safe and is good for holding the soup for serving. If you don't happen to have one, any good 6 quart stovetop soup pot will suffice. If you want to make a smaller amount, just divide the quantities and use a smaller pot. Most of these soups freeze well. The exceptions are the cream soups, which tend to separate when thawed.

SOUPS

SPANISH RICE SOUP

Sue Kerr 2000

This soup was developed by our right-hand-girl, Sue. I like to add 1/4 cup of nutritional yeast for a creamier texture - also good with chicken broth, same reason.

1 onion, chopped
1 bell pepper (red or green)
sauté together in 3 Tbsp.   olive oil
Add:
3 cans of diced tomatoes
1 can of pinto beans
3/4 cup green chilies
1/2 cup chopped cilantro
Garlic chives
2 tsp. cumin
1/2 tsp. Mrs. Dash
1/2 cup rice
Water to make 5 quarts
Heat to simmering, serve

Sue came up with this recipe once when we were wondering what kind of soup to make for the day. We all love it!

SOUPS

TOMATO BASIL SOUP

1 onion, diced
2 red bell peppers, diced
Sauté in 1/2 stick butter and 2 Tbsp. olive oil

Add
2 cups half and half
2 cups milk
1/4 cup nutritional yeast
1/2 tsp. cumin
1/2 tsp. curry
1/2 tsp. Mrs. Dash
3 cans tomato puree
2 cups fresh basil, chopped
Water to make 5 quarts

Heat to simmer and puree, using a hand blender.
Reduce heat and serve

NOTES:

Sharon Young has been part of Cinnamon Sticks for a long time and she really likes this particular soup. She adds some small salad shrimp, a dash of garlic powder and a little more half-and-half to make a fabulous, quick Shrimp Bisque!

SOUPS

VEGGIE SOUP

1 onion, chopped
1 red bell pepper, chopped
Sauté in 3 Tbsp. olive oil
Add:
4 cups shredded cabbage
Stir occasionally until cabbage is soft (5 - 10 minutes)

Add:
1/2 cup carrots, chopped
1 cup potatoes, chopped
2 cans diced tomatoes
1 can tomato sauce
Water to make 5 quarts
1 tsp. Mrs. Dash

Place 8 whole cloves and 6 bay leaves in a large tea strainer (or spice bag) and suspend in the soup

Cook until veggies are tender, remove spices

NOTES:
Cindy Hader was a member of the team practically from the beginning; she came to work at Cinnamon Sticks not long after we opened the tea room. Being a vegetarian, it was easy for her to answer questions about our vegetable-based soups which are usually served on Wednesdays and Fridays (the days Cindy worked). This is one of her favorites.

SOUPS

CHICKEN, RICE AND GREEN BEAN SOUP

1 onion, diced
Sauté in 3 Tbsp. olive oil

Add:
2 quarts of hot water
1 pkg. frozen French cut green beans
1 Tbsp. dried dill
1 tsp. Mrs. Dash
2 Tbsp. chicken broth concentrate
1/2 lb. cooked chicken, chopped
3/4 cup rice

Cook until rice is done, about 20 minutes.
Add hot water to make 5 quarts

Notes:

SOUPS

POTATO LEEK SOUP

3 medium leeks, thoroughly washed and chopped, use only white and light green portion.
1/4 cup butter
3 qts. milk
1/2 tsp. Mrs. Dash
2 cups potatoes, diced
3/4 cup potato flakes for thickener

Sauté leeks in the butter. Add milk and Mrs. Dash, heat to just before boiling. Add potatoes and cook until done. Reduce heat and whisk in potato flakes.

Notes:

SOUPS

POTATO BACON SOUP

1 large onion, diced
Sauté in 2 Tbsp. olive oil and 1/2 stick butter
1/4 lb. cooked bacon, chopped
Add to onions. Continue cooking until bacon is crisp

Reduce heat and add:
3/4 gal. milk
1/2 tsp. Mrs. Dash
1 tsp. dried dill
Salt to taste

When mixture is hot, add 2 cups diced potatoes. Cook until potatoes are done. You can add potato flakes to thicken.

Notes:

SOUPS

SOUTHWESTERN CHICKEN SOUP

1 large onion, chopped
1 red pepper, chopped
Sauté onion and red peppers in 3 Tbsp. olive oil
Add:
2 Tbsp. chicken broth concentrate
1/2 cup fresh cilantro, chopped
1 cup water
1 large can tomato paste (or two small)
Blend with a hand blender.
Add:
1/2 cup carrots, chopped
1 can corn, whole kernel
1 can black beans, drained and rinsed
1 cup potatoes, chopped
1/2 cup green chilies
1 tsp. cumin
1/4 tsp. garlic powder
1/2 lb. chopped chicken (mesquite flavored is good)
1/2 cup tricolor pasta
Water to make 5 quarts

NOTES:

A veggie version of this is good. Just substitute ¼ cup nutritional yeast for the chicken broth and leave out the chicken.

SOUPS

WHITE CHICKEN CHILI

3 Tbsp. olive oil
1/2 lb. cooked white meat chicken, diced
3 cans white beans, drained and rinsed
3/4 cup green chilies
2 tsp. cumin
1 medium onion, chopped
1 red pepper, chopped
1/2 tsp. Mrs. Dash
3 Tbsp. chicken broth concentrate
Water to make 5 quarts

Sauté the onion and red pepper in olive oil. Rinse beans in a colander and add to the onions and peppers. Add all other ingredients and bring to a boil. Reduce heat and serve.

Notes:

SOUPS

BEAN AND PASTA SOUP

3 Tbsp. olive oil
1 medium onion, chopped
1 red pepper, chopped
1 can black beans, drained and rinsed
1 can red beans, drained and rinsed
1 can kidney beans, drained and rinsed
2 cans diced tomatoes
1 can tomato paste
1/2 cup tricolor spiral pasta
Water to make 5 quarts

Sauté onion and pepper in olive oil. Rinse beans in a colander and add to onions/peppers. Add all other ingredients and bring to a boil. Reduce heat and serve.

NOTES:

A little cumin is good in this.

SOUPS

CHICKEN MUSHROOM SOUP

1 medium onion, chopped
1/2 red bell pepper, chopped
1 lb. white mushrooms, chopped
1/2 stick butter
2 cups half and half
2 cups milk
2 Tbsp. chicken broth concentrate
1 lb. cooked white meat chicken, chopped
Milk to make 5 quarts

Sauté onion, pepper and mushrooms in butter. Add half and half and milk. Heat to simmer and stir in chicken broth. Add milk to make 5 quarts. Lower heat, add chicken, serve.

Notes:

SOUPS

CHICKEN NOODLE SOUP

An old-time favorite - good for what ails you!

1 lb. cooked white meat chicken, chopped
3 Tbsp. olive oil
1 medium onion, chopped
2 Tbsp. chicken broth concentrate
1 cup carrots, chopped
1/2 cup parsley, chopped

1 cup bow-tie noodles

Sauté onion in butter. Add 2 quarts water, bring to a boil and add chicken broth concentrate. When dissolved, add all other ingredients except for noodles. Cook until veggies are tender, reduce heat and add noodles. When the noodles are done, add water to make 5 quarts, heat and serve.

Notes:

SOUPS

BAKED POTATO SOUP

2 medium baking potatoes
1 medium onion, chopped
3 Tbsp. olive oil
10 rashers of cooked bacon, chopped
2 qts. milk
1 qt. liquid cheese (like you use for nachos)
chives and sour cream for garnish

Bake the potatoes and allow to cool. Sauté onion in olive oil; add bacon and cook until crisp. Add milk and raise temperature to 180 degrees. Add liquid cheese and whisk until mixture is smooth. Chop cooked potatoes into small pieces and add. Reduce heat and serve. Add chives and a dollop of sour cream for garnish.

NOTES:

This is another one of those serendipity soups - we had a little broccoli cheese soup left over and didn't want to make more, so we added baked potatoes and bacon and..........voila!

SOUPS

Notes:

SOUPS

SEAFOOD CIOPPINO

1 can (28 oz.) diced tomatoes, undrained
2 medium onions, chopped
3 celery ribs, chopped
1 bottle (8 oz.) clam juice
1 can (6 oz.) tomato paste
1/2 cup white wine or vegetable broth
5 cloves garlic, minced
1 Tbsp. red wine vinegar
1 Tbsp. olive oil
1-2 tsp. Italian seasoning
1/2 tsp. sugar
1 bay leaf

1 lb. haddock fillets (or cod) cut into 1" pieces
1 lb. small uncooked shrimp, peeled and deveined
1 can (6 oz.) lump crabmeat, drained
1 can (6 oz.) chopped clams
2 Tbsp. parsley, minced

In a 4-5 quart SLOW COOKER, combine the first 12 ingredients. Cover and cook on low for 4-5 hours. Stir in the fish. Cover and cook for 30 minutes longer or until fish flakes easily with a fork and shrimp turn pink. Stir in the parsley. Discard bay leaf.

Serves 6-8

SOUPS

BLACK BEAN SOUP

1 Tbsp. olive oil
3/4 cup onion, chopped
2 (15 oz.) cans black beans, divided and drained
1 (14 oz.) can fat-free chicken broth
1 (15 oz.) can whole kernel corn, drained
1 (14 oz.) can Mexican-style tomatoes
3 bay leaves
1 tsp. ground ginger
1/2 tsp. thyme
1/2 tsp. ground cumin
1 Tbsp. balsamic vinegar

Saute onion in olive oil. Coarsely mash black beans from one can; leave the second can of beans whole. Combine all ingredients in a medium Dutch oven and simmer for 8-10 minutes. Remove bay leaves.

Makes about 4 servings.

Notes:

SOUPS

CURRIED CARROT SOUP WITH APPLES

1 lb. carrots, peeled and thinly sliced
2 small parsnips, peeled and thinly sliced
1 onion, finely chopped
1 celery stalk, sliced
1 Tbsp. olive oil
1-1/2 tsp. curry powder
1 apple, peeled and chopped
1 thick strip of orange peel
6 cups reduced-sodium chicken broth
Salt and pepper to taste

Mix vegetables with the oil in a large pot over low heat. Cover and cook, stirring often, for 15 minutes or until soft. Stir in the curry powder, season with salt and add remaining ingredients. Bring to a boil, lower heat to a simmer and cook, covered, for 20 minutes. Add salt and pepper; puree soup with a hand blender.

Serve with a dollop of low-fat sour cream and chives, if desired. Makes six servings.

Note: Substitute vegetable broth for a vegetarian soup.

SOUPS

SWEET POTATO-COCONUT SOUP

1-1/2 Tbsp. canola oil
1 small red onion, chopped
2" piece of fresh ginger, grated
Pinch of red-pepper flakes
3 cups low-sodium chicken stock (or vegetable stock)
1/2 cup water
1-1/2 lbs. sweet potatoes, peeled and cut into a large dice
1-1/2 cups unsweetened coconut milk
1 Tbsp. honey
Large pinch of ground cinnamon

Heat oil in a large saucepan over medium heat. Add onion and ginger; cook until soft, about 5 minutes. Add red pepper flakes and cook for 30 seconds. Add stock and water; bring to a boil. Add sweet potatoes; bring to a simmer. Cook until potatoes are soft, 20-30 minutes. Cool for 10 minutes.

Transfer mixture to a blender and process until smooth. Return to saucepan; simmer over low heat. Whisk in coconut milk, honey and cinnamon. Cook until thickened and warmed through. Season with salt and pepper.

Makes four generous servings.

SOUPS

SOUTHWESTERN GAZPACHO

1 (15 oz) jar of roasted red peppers
1 can diced tomatoes
1/2 cup red-wine vinegar
1/4 cup olive oil
1/4 cup onion, chopped
1 seedless cucumber, peeled and chopped
2 carrots, peeled and chopped
1 celery stalk, chopped
1 green bell pepper, cored, seeded and chopped
Salt and freshly ground black pepper, to taste
Hot sauce, to taste (optional)
2 Tbsp. fresh cilantro or parsley, chopped
1 avocado, seeded, peeled and diced
2 hard-cooked eggs, chopped

Place the roasted red peppers and tomatoes in a blender and process until smooth. Transfer to a mixing bowl and add the vinegar, olive oil, onion, cucumber, carrots, celery and green bell pepper. Process in small batches in the blender until blended but still slightly chunky. Refrigerate until well chilled; at least 3 hours. Adjust the seasoning with salt, pepper and optional hot sauce. Stir in the cilantro or parsley just before serving. Garnish with chopped avocado and hard-cooked eggs. Serves 4-6.

Note: This is a wonderful summer soup, because it is served cold. Easy and really refreshing.

SOUPS

CURRIED ONION SOUP

4 Tbsp. butter
4 cups onion, finely chopped
1 Tbsp. curry powder
1/4 cup flour
6-8 cups chicken, beef or vegetable stock or milk
Salt and black pepper to taste
1/2 cup sour cream

Heat butter in a large pot, sauté the onions until tender but not browned (about 10 minutes).
Stir in the curry powder; cook 1 minute.
Whisk in flour; cook for about 3 minutes.
Add the liquid and bring to a simmer, stirring frequently.
Adjust the salt and pepper and simmer for 10 minutes.
Remove from heat and add sour cream.
Puree with hand blender if desired.

Serves 6-8

SOUPS

CHICKEN AVOCADO SOUP WITH FRIED TORTILLAS

3-1/2 Tbsp. cooking oil
4-6" corn tortillas, halved and cut crosswise into ¼" strips
1 clove of garlic
1 jalapeno chili, seeds and ribs removed
2 ripe avocados, skin and seeds removed
1 Tbsp. lime juice
1/4 tsp. Tabasco sauce, plus more to taste
3-1/2 cups water
1 tsp. salt
1/4 tsp. black pepper
1 onion, chopped
3 cups low-sodium chicken broth or homemade stock
1 lb. boneless, skinless chicken breasts (about 3) cut to bite size

In a large pot, heat 2 tbsp. of the oil over moderately high heat. Add the tortilla strips and cook, stirring frequently, until brown and crisp (3-4 minutes).   Remove the tortillas and drain on paper towels.

In a blender, combine the garlic, jalapeno, avocados, lime juice and Tabasco, 1-1/2 cups of the water, 1/2 tsp. of the salt, and the black pepper. Puree until smooth.

Heat the remaining 1-1/2 Tbsp. of oil in the pot over medium heat. Add the onion and cook, stirring frequently, until translucent (about 5 minutes).
Add the broth and the remaining 2 cups of water and the remaining salt. Bring to a simmer.

SOUPS

Stir the chicken into the pot; cook until done (about 5 minutes). Add the avocado puree. Heat through (about 2 minutes). Serve topped with the crisp tortilla strips.

Note: If you don't want to go to the trouble of making your own tortilla strips, you can substitute broken up purchased tortilla chips.

Serves 4.

SOUPS

ENTREES

ENTREES

CHICKEN POT PIE

Note: this is replacing a recipe for the chicken pot pie we served in the tea room. It's easier and every bit as good.

Preheat oven to 425 degrees

1 lb. frozen chicken breast strips, thawed
1 large package frozen peas and carrots
1/2 cup celery, sliced
1/3 cup unsalted butter
1/3 cup onion, chopped
1/3 cup flour
1/2 tsp. salt
1/4 tsp. black pepper
1-3/4 cups low-sodium chicken broth
2/3 cup milk
2 (9") unbaked pie crusts

In a saucepan over medium heat, cook onions in butter until softened. Stir in flour, salt and pepper. Slowly stir in chicken broth and milk. Simmer over medium-low heat until thickened. Remove from heat and set aside.

Line a 10" pie pan with one of the pie crusts. Put the chicken and vegetables into the pie crust. Pour the hot liquid mixture over the top. Cover with top crust, seal edges and cut away excess dough. Make several small slits in the top to allow steam to escape.

Bake for 30-35 minutes or until pastry is golden brown and filling is bubbly. Cool for 10 minutes before serving. Serves 6.

ENTREES

OLD-FASHIONED GLAZED MEATLOAF

Preheat oven to 375 degrees

For the meatloaf:
1 lb. ground beef or turkey
1/4 lb. ground pork sausage (optional)
1 6 oz. can tomato paste
1/2 cup onion, chopped
1/2 cup green bell pepper, chopped
1/2 cup quick-cooking oats
1 egg, lightly beaten
1 tsp. salt
1/4 tsp. pepper

For the glaze:
1/3 cup ketchup
2 Tbsp. light brown sugar, packed
1 Tbsp. mustard

In a large bowl, combine ground meat, tomato paste, onion, green pepper, oats, egg, salt and pepper. Shape mixture into a loaf on foil lined sheet pan or use a 9x5 loaf pan.

In a small bowl, whisk together the ketchup, brown sugar and mustard. Coat the top of the meatloaf with the glaze. Bake for 1 hour or until meatloaf is firm and cooked through. Serve hot.

Makes 6-8 servings.

ENTREES

ITALIAN EGGPLANT PARMIGIANA

A favorite of mine for many years. It takes some time and has quite a few steps (translation: several bowls, dishes, etc. to wash) but don't let that stop you from trying it.

Preheat oven to 350 degrees

1 large eggplant
Salt and ground pepper to taste
1 cup fine dry bread crumbs
2 eggs, slightly beaten
Olive oil
1-1/2 cups tomato sauce, heated
1/2 lb. Mozzarella cheese, sliced
1 tsp. dried basil, crumbled
1/4 cup Parmesan cheese, grated

Wash eggplant and cut crosswise into 1/4" thick rounds. Do not peel. Season with salt and pepper. Dip each slice into bread crumbs, dip into egg, and then again into bread crumbs. (Depending on the size of the eggplant, more bread crumbs and egg may be necessary.) Place in refrigerator for 30 minutes.
Heat about 1/8" of oil in a skillet. Fry eggplant slices until tender and golden on both sides. Drain on paper towel. Line a large buttered shallow baking dish with some of the tomato sauce. Arrange a layer of eggplant slices over the sauce. Cover with a layer of Mozzarella slices, more sauce, and a sprinkling of basil and Parmesan. Repeat in layers until the dish is full. Bake in 350 degree oven for 25-30 minutes. Makes 6 servings.

ENTREES

I have recently simplified this recipe!! I coat the eggplant slices with the egg/bread crumb mixture and place them in a single layer on a large cookie sheet that has been lightly seasoned with olive oil. Place the cookie sheet in a 375 degree oven for 25-30 minutes, turning the eggplant slices once at the half way point. This is not only easier, it also eliminates a lot of oil so it's healthier. It also gets rid of a messy skillet!

ENTREES

QUICHE

Preheat oven to 400 degrees

9" unbaked pie shell
1-1/2 cups Swiss cheese, grated
1 Tbsp. flour, sifted
3 eggs
1 cup milk
1/2 cup light cream
(or 1 cup evaporated milk in place of milk and cream)
1/2 tsp. salt

Brush unbaked pie shell with a little egg white. Bake for 5 minutes at 400 degrees. Mix cheese and flour; spread in partially baked pie shell. Top with whatever fillings you select (see NOTE). Beat eggs lightly; add milk and cream (or evaporated milk) and seasonings. Pour into pastry and shake gently to settle liquid. Bake at 400 degrees for 25-30 minutes or until tester comes out clean.

NOTES:

A variety of fillings can be used. Spinach (frozen, well drained) and mushroom. Bacon, fried crisp, drained and broken into pieces and onion, in rings or chopped into large pieces and sautéed in butter. Cheddar cheese, grated, combined with the Swiss cheese. A mixture of chopped and sautéed vegetables; green and red bell pepper, zucchini, mushroom, onion or any other fresh vegetables.

Serves 6. Have fun creating your own variations.

ENTREES

QUICHE (No milk recipe)

Preheat oven to 375 degrees

4 eggs, beaten
1 cup cheese, Jack or Swiss, grated

Whatever fillings you want:
    Shrimp
    Crab
    Spinach
    Mushrooms
    Onions

Combine ingredients in an unbaked 9" pie shell. Bake at 375 degrees for 25-30 minutes or until tested comes out clean.

Notes:

ENTREES

CHICKEN AND SMOKED SAUSAGE GUMBO

3 Tbsp. cooking oil
3 Tbsp. flour
1 onion, chopped
2 ribs celery, chopped
1 green bell pepper, chopped
1 10 oz. package frozen sliced okra
1 bay leaf
1-1/2 tsp. dried thyme
1 tsp. dried oregano
1 tsp. salt
1/4 tsp. black pepper
1/4 tsp. cayenne
1-15 oz. crushed, canned tomatoes in thick puree
1 quart low-sodium chicken broth or homemade stock
1/2 lb. smoked sausage, halved lengthwise, cut into 1/4 " pieces
1 lb. boneless, skinless chicken breasts, cut into 3/4" slices

In a LARGE stainless-steel pot, heat the oil on medium high. Add the flour and cook, whisking continually, until it starts to brown (about 4 minutes). Reduce the heat to moderate low setting. Stir in the onion, celery and bell pepper. Cook until they start to soften (about 7 minutes). Add the okra, bay leaf, thyme, oregano, salt, black pepper, cayenne and tomatoes. Cover and cook for 5 minutes.
Stir in the broth and smoked sausage. Bring to a boil. Reduce heat and simmer for 15 minutes. Add the chicken and cook until just done, 4-5 minutes longer. Remove the bay leaf.

Serve over rice if desired.

ENTREES

MINI CHILE RELLENO CASSEROLES

Preheat oven to 400 degrees

2 (4oz) cans diced green chilies, drained and patted dry
3/4 cup frozen corn, thawed and patted dry
4 scallions, thinly sliced
1 cup shredded reduced-fat Cheddar cheese
1-1/2 cups nonfat milk
6 large egg whites
4 large eggs
1/4 tsp. salt

Coat eight 6 oz. or four 10 oz. heatproof ramekins with cooking spray and place on large baking sheet.

Equally divide the green chilies, corn and scallions among the ramekins. Top each with cheese. Whisk milk, egg whites, eggs and salt in a medium bowl until combined. Divide the egg mixture evenly among the ramekins.

Bake the mini casseroles until the tops begin to brown and the eggs are set; about 25 minutes for 6 oz. ramekins and about 35 minutes for 10 oz. ramekins.

Variation: add a small can of artichoke hearts, chopped into bite-size pieces.

ENTREES

SLOW COOKER BEEF STROGANOFF

2 lbs. beef stew meat, cut into 1" cubes
1 package (8 oz.) mushrooms, halved or sliced
1/2 cup onion, chopped
1 package beef stroganoff seasoning
1 cup water
1 cup sour cream

Place meat, mushrooms and onion in slow cooker.
Mix seasoning packet and water until blended. Pour over meat and vegetables and toss to coat well. Cover
Cook 8 hours on LOW or 4 hours on HIGH. Stir in sour cream until well blended. Cover. Cook 10 minutes longer on LOW. Serve over cooked egg noodles or rice.

Notes:

ENTREES

CHICKEN BREASTS WITH BACON

Preheat oven to 400 degrees

8 bacon strips
4 boneless, skinless chicken breast halves
1 Tbsp. olive oil
1/2 tsp. salt
1/4 tsp. black pepper
2 Roma tomatoes, sliced
6 fresh basil leaves, thinly sliced
4 slices part-skim mozzarella cheese

Place bacon on a foil-lined baking sheet. Bake for 8-10 minutes or until partially cooked but not crisp. Remove to paper towels and drain well.

Place chicken breasts in an ungreased 13"X9" baking dish; brush with olive oil and sprinkle with salt and pepper. Top with tomatoes and basil. Crisscross each chicken breast with two bacon strips.

Bake uncovered for 20-25 minutes or until a meat thermometer reads 170. Top with cheese slices; bake 1 minute longer or until cheese is melted.

Serves 4

Note: I have used Havarti cheese instead of the mozzarella and it's very good that way. This smells wonderful cooking!!

ENTREES

ZUCCHINI PIE

Preheat oven to 350 degrees

2 cups zucchini, shredded
3/4 cup biscuit mix
3/4 cup cheddar cheese, shredded
1 small onion, chopped
1/2 tsp. salt
1/4 tsp. pepper
1/4 tsp. rubbed sage
2 large eggs, lightly beaten
1/4 cup vegetable oil

Stir all ingredients together. Pour into a greased 9" pie pan. Bake for 45 minutes. Cool for 10 minutes. Serves 6.

Note: Sometimes I use 1 cup of zucchini and 1 cup of yellow squash. I also add things like chopped fresh mushrooms and pimentos or roasted red bell peppers. You could also add fresh or dried herbs.

Notes:

ENTREES

TEX-MEX QUICHE

Preheat oven to 325 degrees

1 tsp. chili powder
1 unbaked pie shell (9")
1 cup (4 oz.) shredded Cheddar cheese
1 cup (4 oz.) shredded Monterey Jack cheese
1 Tbsp. flour
3 eggs, beaten
1-1/2 cups half-and-half cream
1 can (4 oz.) green chilies, well drained and chopped
1 small can ripe olives, well drained and sliced
1 tsp. salt
1/4 tsp. pepper

Sprinkle chili powder over the inside of the pie shell. Combine cheeses with flour and place in pie shell.

Combine eggs, half-and-half, chilies, olives, and salt and pepper. Pour over cheese.

Bake for 45-55 minutes or until a knife inserted in the center comes out clean. Cool for 10 minutes before cutting into wedges.

Yield: 6 servings

ENTREES

NEW MEXICO STYLE GREEN CHILI STEW

(Be careful how many hot chilies you use!)

6-7 Hatch chilies (Anaheim will work too)
2 lbs. lean pork loin or beef
2 Tbsp. vegetable oil
1/2 cup onion, finely chopped
1 garlic clove, minced
2 jalapenos, diced
6 cups chicken broth
6 oz. beer (optional)
1/2 tsp. oregano
1/2 tsp. salt
1 tsp. pepper
3 bay leaves
1/2 tsp. cumin
1 (10 oz.) can diced tomatoes
3 large potatoes
2 Tbsp. flour
2 Tbsp. butter

Use Hatch chilies that have been roasted and had skins removed. Cube the meat, sprinkle with salt and pepper and brown with onions and garlic in oil in a large pot for about 5 minutes. Add jalapeno, broth, (half a can of beer if using), and spices. Bring to a simmer.

Add the chopped Hatch chilies. Let simmer for 30 minutes. Add tomatoes and potatoes along with a cup of hot water if more liquid is needed. Simmer until potatoes are done.

Melt butter in a small skillet and whisk in flour. Cook for 2 minutes, stirring constantly. Add to the pot to thicken.

ENTREES

ZUCCHINI, CORN, BLACK BEAN QUESADILLAS

Preheat oven to 200 degrees

1 small zucchini, grated, drained on paper towels (~1 cup)
1 cup frozen corn, thawed and drained on paper towels
1 small red onion, chopped
1 jalapeno chili, seeds and ribs removed, chopped
1-2/3 cups black beans, drained and rinsed (15 oz. can)
1/2 tsp. salt
1/4 freshly ground pepper
1 tsp. chili powder
3/4 pound Monterey Jack cheese, grated

8 large (burrito-size) flour tortillas
2 Tbsp. canola oil

In a large bowl, combine the zucchini, corn, onion, jalapeno, beans, salt, pepper and chili powder. Mix well and then stir in the cheese.

Put about 1/3 cup of the filling on one half of each tortilla. Spread the filling to the edge and then fold the tortilla over the filling. In a large skillet, heat 1/2 Tbsp. of the oil over moderate heat. Add 2 of the quesadillas to the pan and cook, turning once, until the cheese melts (~1-1/2 minutes per side). Remove from pan and keep warm on a baking sheet in the oven. Repeat in batches with remaining oil and quesadillas; cut into wedges and serve.

Add shredded, cooked chicken if you wish. These make great appetizers as well as a hardy meal. Good served with sour cream and guacamole.

ENTREES

SPAGHETTI WITH TOMATOES, BASIL, OLIVES AND CHEESE

2 lbs. (about 6) tomatoes, chopped (this is an ideal summer dish when tomatoes are at their best)
3/4 lb. salted fresh mozzarella cheese, at room temperature, cut into 1/2" cubes
1-1/4 cups fresh basil, chopped
1/2 cup black olives, halved
4 tsp. balsamic vinegar
1-1/4 tsp salt
1/2 tsp black pepper

1 lb. spaghetti
1/2 cup olive oil
3 cloves garlic, minced

In a large glass or stainless steel bowl, combine the chopped tomatoes with the fresh mozzarella cheese, basil, olives, balsamic vinegar, salt and black pepper.

Cook spaghetti according to directions on package. Drain. Add to the tomato mixture and toss. Heat the oil in a small frying pan of moderate low heat. Add the garlic and cook, stirring for 1 minute. Pour the oil and garlic over the pasta and toss again.

Variations: Add some drained capers, chopped red onion, or grated Parmesan to the pasta.

ENTREES

MOROCCAN STEW WITH COUSCOUS

2 Tbsp. olive oil
1 cup onion, chopped
2 tsp. fresh ginger root, finely chopped
1-1/2 tsp. garlic clove, finely chopped
2 tsp. curry powder
1/2 tsp. salt
2 cups eggplant cut in 3/4" cubes
2 cups ripe tomatoes, chopped (Romas are best)
2 cups zucchini, sliced 1/4" thick and cut in half
1 cup mushrooms, sliced
3/4 cup water
1/2 cup raisins
2 Tbsp. fresh cilantro, chopped
1 Tbsp. jalapeno or serrano pepper (optional)

2 cups cooked couscous or rice

In Dutch oven combine oil, onion, ginger root and garlic. Cook over medium heat, stirring occasionally, until onion is softened (5 to 6 minutes). Add curry powder and salt; continue cooking, stirring constantly, 1 minute. Add all remaining ingredients except raisins, cilantro and couscous. Bring to a boil. Cover; reduce heat to medium-low. Cook, stirring occasionally, until vegetables are tender (20-25 minutes). Stir in raisins and cilantro. Continue cooking until heated through (3-4 minutes). Season to taste. Serve with cooked couscous. Makes 4-6 servings.

ENTREES

QUICK LEMON SHRIMP SCAMPI

3/4 lb. large shrimp, cleaned and deveined
1 Tbsp. olive oil
2 Tbsp. minced garlic
2/3 cup low sodium chicken broth
1 Tbsp. fresh lemon juice
1 Tbsp. lemon pepper
5 Tbsp. butter
Chopped parsley and lemon slices for garnish (opt.)

Heat oil in non-stick skillet. Saute garlic 1-2 minutes until soft but not browned. Add shrimp; cook 1 minute. Add broth, lemon juice, lemon pepper and butter; increase heat and boil about 2 minutes. Serve over rice and garnish with parsley and lemon slices if you wish.

NOTES:

Prepare your rice before you start the scampi because it cooks very quickly. This recipe will serve 2-3 people.

You can substitute vegetable broth for chicken broth.

ENTREES

BLACK BEAN CHILI

1 Tbsp. olive oil
1 cup onion, finely chopped
2 garlic cloves, minced
1/2 cup carrot, finely chopped
1 large red bell pepper, seeded and finely chopped
1 Tbsp. chili powder
1 tsp. ground cumin
1 (14 1/2 oz.) can diced tomatoes, undrained
2 (15 oz.) cans black beans, drained and rinsed
1/4 cup canned chopped green chilies
3/4 cup water
3/4 cup orange juice
1/4 tsp. salt
2 Tbsp. cilantro, chopped (optional)
1-2 Tbsp. shredded Cheddar cheese for each serving (optional)

In a Dutch oven, heat the olive oil over medium heat. When hot, add the onion, garlic, carrot and bell pepper. Sauté for 5 minutes. Stir in the chili powder, cumin, undrained tomatoes, black beans, green chilies, water, orange juice and salt. Bring to a boil, reduce heat to medium-low and simmer 20 minutes, stirring often to prevent sticking. Stir in the cilantro and garnish each serving with cheese if desired. Makes 4 servings.

Note: Stir in 1-2 Tbsp. nutritional yeast for a creamier base.

ENTREES

BLACK BEAN BURGERS

3 (15 oz.) cans black beans, drained and rinsed
1-1/2 cups uncooked oatmeal
1 medium onion, diced
2 jalapeno or serrano peppers, seeded and diced
3/4 cup fresh cilantro, chopped
2 eggs, lightly beaten
1 tsp. salt
1/4 cup flour
1/4 cup cornmeal
1 Tbsp. vegetable oil

Coarsely mash beans with a fork. Combine with oatmeal, onion, jalapeno peppers, cilantro, eggs and salt. Shape into 8 patties.

Stir together flour and cornmeal; dredge patties in mixture. Cook in hot oil over medium heat for about 5 minutes on each side or until lightly browned. Serve on hamburger buns if desired.

NOTES:

An interesting alternative to meat burgers.

ENTREES

SALMON WITH PECAN COATING

Preheat oven to 400 degrees

2 Tbsp. Dijon-style mustard
2 Tbsp. butter, melted
4 tsp. honey
1/4 cup fresh bread crumbs
1/4 cup pecans, finely chopped
2 tsp. fresh parsley, chopped
4 (4-6oz each) salmon fillets or steaks, thawed
Lemon pepper

In a small bowl, mix together mustard, butter and honey; set aside. In another small bowl, mix together bread crumbs, pecans and parsley; set aside. Season each salmon fillet or steak with lemon pepper. Place on a lightly greased baking sheet or broiling pan. Brush each filet or steak with mustard/honey mixture and pat top with bread crumb/pecan mixture. Bake for 10 minutes per inch of thickness, measured at thickest part, or until salmon just flakes when tested with a fork. Makes four servings.

This is my favorite way to prepare salmon when I cook it inside... I also love Paul's grilled salmon when I can talk him into cooking outside!

GENERAL NOTE: I heard a really great suggestion that I have to pass along....when you are spraying a pan with oil, open your dish washer and spray over the inside of the door. Next time you turn on the dish washer the door will get cleaned and you won't have an overspray of oil on your kitchen counter or sink.

ENTREES

ROASTED PORK LOIN WITH ORANGE-CHILI GLAZE

Preheat oven to 350 degrees

1 center-cut pork loin, 4-5 pounds
Salt and pepper (freshly ground) to taste

Orange-Chili Glaze:
2 Tbsp. chili powder
1 Tbsp. ground cumin
1 Tbsp. ground coriander
1/2 Tbsp. ground cinnamon
1 cup orange juice (fresh squeezed)
2 Tbsp. orange zest
1/2 cup cider vinegar
2 Tbsp. serrano chili, seeded and finely chopped
1/2 cup sugar
1/4 cup molasses

Put pork loin on a rack in a shallow roasting pan and sprinkle lightly with salt and generously with pepper. Roast uncovered for 1 hour.

In a saucepan combine chili powder, cumin, coriander and cinnamon, and toast over medium heat for 2-3 minutes, stirring constantly, until spices begin to smoke and become fragrant. Immediately remove from heat. Add orange juice, vinegar, chilis, sugar and molasses; stir well and return to heat

Bring to a boil, reduce heat and simmer for about 45 minutes, stirring occasionally, until thickened. Remove pork roast from oven and spoon the pan drippings over the

ENTREES

meat. Brush glaze generously over the pork. Cook for 45-60 minutes longer, basting with the glaze, until a thermometer inserted into the thickest part of the roast registers 160 degrees. Let meat rest for about 15 minutes. Cut into 1/2" thick slices and serve hot. Makes 6-8 servings depending on size of roast.

This is a terrific way to cook pork loin. It's easy and really delicious.

ENTREES

MEXICAN LASAGNA

Preheat oven to 350 degrees

2 lbs. ground beef or ground turkey
1 can (16 oz.) refried beans
1 can (4 oz.) chopped green chilies
1 envelope taco seasoning
2 Tbsp. hot salsa

4 cups (16 oz.) shredded Mexican blend cheese (divided)
12 oz. uncooked lasagna noodles (no-boil variety)
1 jar (16 oz.) mild salsa
2 cups water
2 cups (16 oz.) sour cream
1 can (2 1/4 oz.) sliced ripe olives, drained
3 green onions, chopped
1 medium tomato, chopped (optional)

In a large skillet, cook ground meat over medium heat until no longer pink; drain. Stir in the refried beans, chilies, taco seasoning and hot salsa.
In a greased 13"x9" baking pan, layer a third of the noodles and meat mixture. Sprinkle with 1 cup of cheese. Repeat layers twice. Combine mild salsa with water and pour over the top. Cover and bake for 1 hour.

Top with sour cream, olives, onions and tomatoes (if desired) and remaining cup of cheese. Bake, uncovered 5 minutes longer. Let stand for 10-15 minutes before cutting.

ENTREES

GINGER CHICKEN

2-3 lbs. skinless, boneless chicken breasts
1 cup plain yogurt
1/4 cup lemon juice, fresh squeezed
1/4 cup vegetable oil
6 cloves garlic, coarsely chopped
A 2-inch piece of ginger root, peeled and coarsely chopped
1 tsp. Cayenne pepper, or to taste
Salt and freshly ground pepper to taste

Cut each piece of chicken crosswise into 3 pieces and place in a bowl. Combine the remaining ingredients in an electric blender or food processor and blend until smooth. Pour over the chicken pieces and toss to coat thoroughly. Let stand at room temperature for 1-2 hours. Saute the chicken pieces in small batches in a heavy skillet over high heat until golden brown on all sides, about 10 minutes, adding more marinade to the skillet as you add chicken pieces. BE SURE the marinade is cooked thoroughly since it has been sitting in contact with the raw chicken. Watch to prevent sticking. Serve immediately. Serves 4-6.

Notes: Chicken breast tenders work well for this recipe. When I make this for 2 people I use 1 lb. of chicken but I do the same amount of marinade (when you taste it you'll know why!) This is a very spicy dish. If you want to tone it down a bit, decrease the amount of cayenne pepper. You also don't have to use so many garlic cloves if you prefer not to. Usually marinades are not used in the cooking process but this one definitely should be and remember to cook the chicken and the marinade thoroughly. Serve the chicken with its ginger sauce over rice.

ENTREES

STUFFED CABBAGE ROLLS

1 head cabbage
1 lb. ground beef or ground turkey
1 egg
1/2 onion, grated
1 carrot. grated
1-2 cloves garlic, crushed
1/2 cup cooked rice
1-2 tsp. seasoning like Mrs. Dash

Sauce:

8 oz. can tomato sauce
1/4 cup cider vinegar
3/4 cup brown sugar, packed

Remove the large outside leaves from the cabbage and wilt them. Mix the next seven ingredients together and roll into walnut sized balls. Place one ball in the middle of each wilted cabbage leaf: roll leaf around the ball to enclose it. Arrange rolls in a large non-stick skillet. If you don't have a skillet large enough to accommodate all of the cabbage rolls in one layer, separate into two skillets. Mix together sauce ingredients and pour over the cabbage rolls. Simmer on medium-low heat for about 1 hour. Recipe should make about 20 cabbage rolls.

ENTREES

Notes

To wilt the cabbage leaves: Fill a large pot with water and bring to a boil; turn off heat. Place a few cabbage leaves at a time into the hot water, leaving them in for about one minute until they start getting soft. Remove with tongs and lay out on paper towel to drain. Continue until you have all the leaves wilted. Let them cool for a few minutes so they will be comfortable to work with.

I keep a kettle of water heated on the stove so that I can add a little water to the skillet now and then to keep the sauce from drying out too much.

I really prefer using ground turkey for this recipe. In fact, I use it for things like chili and spaghetti sauce too. The flavor is very much like ground beef and I think it's a lot safer and healthier.

ENTREES

CHICKEN ENCHILADAS

Preheat oven to 350 degrees

1/4 cup onion, chopped
2 garlic cloves, minced
1 Tbsp. butter
2 Tbsp. flour
1 cup low-sodium chicken broth
1-4 oz. can chopped green chilies
1/4 tsp. ground coriander
1/8 tsp. pepper
1 cup cheddar cheese, shredded (divided)
1/2 cup sour cream
2 cups chopped cooked chicken
4-8" flour tortillas

In a saucepan, sauté onion and garlic in butter until tender. Combine flour and broth until smooth; gradually add to pan. Stir in the chilies, coriander and pepper. Bring to a boil; cook and stir for 2 minutes or until thickened. Remove from heat and stir in 1/2 cup of the shredded cheese and the sour cream until cheese melts.

Combine chicken and 3/4 cup of the sauce. Place about 1/2 cup of the chicken mixture down the center of each tortilla. Roll up and place seam side down in a greased 11x7 baking dish. Pour remaining sauce over the enchiladas.

Bake uncovered for about 20 minutes. Sprinkle with remaining cheese. Bake 5-10 minutes longer or until cheese is melted.

ENTREES

Notes:

ENTREES

SOUTHWESTERN SHEPHERD'S PIE

Preheat oven to 400 degrees

2 Tbsp. olive oil
1 medium onion, diced
1 small green bell pepper, diced
1 Tbsp. garlic, minced
1 Tbsp. green jalapeno, diced
1 lb. ground beef or turkey
1 Tbsp. tomato paste
1 Tbsp. chili powder
1 tsp. ground cumin
1/2 tsp. ground cinnamon
Salt and pepper to taste
2 cups tomatoes, chopped
1/2 cup cooked corn
1/2 cup black beans, rinsed
1/4 cup cilantro, chopped

1-1/2 lbs. sweet potatoes, peeled and cut into chunks
2 Tbsp. butter
1/2 cup milk

Place sweet potatoes in a saucepan with water to cover. Bring to a boil, reduce heat and simmer for 30 minutes. Drain; mash with butter and milk.

Heat oil in large pot over medium heat. Add onion and bell pepper; cook, stirring for 10 minutes. Add garlic and jalapeno, cook for 2 minutes. Raise heat to medium-high; add beef or turkey and brown for 5 minutes. Add tomato paste and spices; cook, stirring, for 2 minutes. Add tomatoes; simmer until liquid reduces (about 15 minutes).

ENTREES

Add corn, beans and 4 Tbsp. of the cilantro. Spoon into a 9x9 baking dish. Spread mashed sweet potatoes over the meat mixture. Bake about 30 minutes, until brown. Garnish with more cilantro. Serves 4. Also good using leftover roast beef or pork.

Notes:

ENTREES

SLOW COOKER PORK CHOPS

3/4 cup all-purpose flour, DIVIDED
1/2 tsp. ground mustard
1/2 tsp. garlic pepper blend
1/4 tsp. seasoned salt
4 boneless pork loin chops (1/2" thick-4 oz. each)
2 Tbsp. canola oil
1 can (14 oz.) chicken broth
1 large onion, sliced into rings (optional)
1 tart apple, sliced into rings (optional)

In a large resealable plastic bag, combine 1/2 cup flour, mustard, pepper blend and seasoned salt. Add chops, one at a time, and shake to coat. In a large skillet, brown meat in oil on both sides.

Transfer to a 5 qt. slow cooker along with onion rings or apple rings, if using. Place remaining flour in a small bowl; whisk in broth until smooth. Pour over chops. Cover and cook on low for 3-4 hours or until meat is tender.

Remove pork to a serving plate and keep warm. Whisk pan juices until smooth; serve with pork.

ENTREES

SLOW COOKER CRANBERRY CHICKEN

1 whole chicken, cut up, OR chicken pieces to equal 3-4 lbs.
1 can (14 oz.) whole-berry cranberry sauce
1 cup barbeque sauce
1 small onion, finely chopped
1 celery rib, finely chopped
1/2 tsp. salt
1/4 tsp. pepper
Hot cooked rice

Place chicken in a 4-5 qt. slow cooker. In a small bowl, combine the cranberry sauce, barbeque sauce, onion, celery, salt and pepper; pour over chicken. Cover and cook on low for 5-6 hours or until chicken is tender.

Serve over hot cooked rice.

Yield: about 6 servings

Note: Try this recipe using pork chops instead of chicken

ENTREES

ZESTY LEMON PEPPER CHICKEN

(This must marinate for 12 hours or overnight)

Preheat oven to 500 degrees when ready to cook

4 chicken breasts or other chicken pieces
3 lemons
1 medium onion
3 Tbsp. olive oil
1 Tbsp. minced garlic
1 tsp. paprika
1 tsp. dried thyme
1/2 tsp. salt
2 Tbsp. freshly ground pepper

Place chicken pieces in large bowl. In a separate bowl, zest the lemons, then juice the lemons. Mince the onion and add it to the bowl along with olive oil, paprika, thyme, salt and pepper. Reserve 3 Tbsp. of the marinade.

Pour marinade over chicken pieces and coat thoroughly. Marinate in refrigerator for 12 hours or overnight.

Put chicken, skin side up, on a shallow roasting pan. Put lemon rinds into the pan. Put chicken in oven and REDUCE HEAT TO 375 DEGREES. Bake for 25 minutes or until chicken is cooked through, brushing with the reserved marinade.

Discard lemon rinds. Serve with remaining marinade. Good over rice.

ENTREES

LEMON BAKED CHICKEN

(make sauce first and chill for at least 30 minutes)

Preheat oven to 350 degrees

1-1/2 lbs. chicken breasts (with bone)
Small amount of flour, seasoned with salt and pepper
2 Tbsp. butter

Sauce:
3 tsp. soy sauce
1/2 cup freshly squeezed lemon juice
1 garlic clove, crushed
1 Tbsp. olive oil

Mix the sauce ingredients well and chill for at least 30 minutes before using.

In a plastic bag, toss the chicken in the seasoned flour to coat. Grease a large ovenproof dish and arrange chicken in a single layer. Melt butter and spoon over chicken. Bake uncovered for 25 minutes.

Turn chicken over, spoon on the lemon sauce and return to oven for another 20 minutes, basting occasionally.

Good served over rice.

Yield: 4-6 servings

ENTREES

CHICKEN PICCATA

4 boneless, skinless chicken breast halves (~1 lb)
1/4 cup flour
1/8 tsp. salt
1/8 tsp. pepper
3 Tbsp. butter
1/4 cup chicken broth
1/4 cup white wine or chicken broth
1 jar (3.5 oz) capers
1 Tbsp. lemon zest, finely shredded
2 Tbsp. freshly squeezed lemon juice
2 Tbsp. fresh parsley, chopped

Rinse chicken, pat dry. Place each breast half between 2 pieces of plastic wrap. Working from the center to the edges, pound chicken lightly with the flat side of a meat mallet to a 1/4" thickness. Remove from plastic wrap.

In a shallow dish or plastic bag, put flour, salt and pepper. Coat each breast with flour mixture; shake off excess.

In a 12" skillet, melt half of the butter. Add chicken and cook over medium-high heat for 4-6 minutes or until tender and no pink remains, turning once. Remove chicken from skillet; keep warm. In the same skillet, combine the chicken broth, wine, capers, lemon peel and lemon juice. Bring to a boil; cook until sauce is reduced to about 1/3 cup. Remove from heat and stir in parsley.

Place chicken in serving dish and pour sauce over top. Good served with rice.

Yield: 4 servings

ENTREES

Notes:

SIDES

SIDES

SLOW-COOKED SQUASH WITH BUTTER & BASIL

2 Tbsp. unsalted butter
1 small onion, diced
Kosher salt
4 cups yellow squash (about 5 medium) cut into 1/4" cubes
10 fresh basil leaves, torn into strips

In a heavy saucepan over <u>very</u> low heat, melt 1 Tbsp. of the butter. Add the onion and season with 1/2 tsp. salt. Cover the pan with a tight-fitting lid and slowly sauté, stirring occasionally, until the onions are translucent and tender (about 6-8 minutes). If at any time the onions begin to brown, add 1 Tbsp. water.

Add remaining Tbsp. of butter and squash and season with 1 tsp. salt. Cover and cook, stirring often, for 15 minutes, until the squash is tender and beginning to fall apart but still has its bright yellow color. Add the basil and immediately stir it in to prevent the steam from turning it black. Cover and cook for a couple minutes more, until the basil is wilted.

SIDES

SWEET ONION CASSEROLE

Preheat oven to 320 degrees

4 large sweet onions, sliced into 1/4" rings
1/4 cup butter
1/4 cup sour cream
3/4 cup grated Parmesan cheese
12 butter-flavored crackers, crushed

Grease a 1 quart baking dish with butter. In a large skillet, sauté onions in butter over medium heat until tender. Remove skillet from heat; stir in sour cream. Spoon half of the onions into the prepared baking dish; sprinkle with Parmesan cheese. Top with the remaining onions and cracker crumbs.

Bake uncovered 20-25 minutes. Serves 4-6.

Notes:

If you like onions you will really love this!

It makes a terrific side dish for almost any entree. Vidalia or 1015 onions work well for this casserole. You can use something other than a sweet onion but it won't be quite as good.

If you don't have butter flavored crackers use plain saltine type crackers. Crush them and put them into the skillet after you've removed the onions...stir them around to soak up the remaining butter.

Notes:

SIDES

MARINATED ASPARAGUS

2 lbs. fresh asparagus, tough ends chopped off
3/4 cup olive oil
1 Tbsp. sugar
1/2 cup white balsamic vinegar (or red if you don't have the white)
4 garlic cloves
1 tsp. red pepper flakes

Boil asparagus for 3 minutes, or until crisp-tender; drain. Blanch asparagus by plunging it into an ice water bath; drain. Arrange asparagus in a 13"X9" baking dish.

Whisk together olive oil, sugar balsamic vinegar, garlic and red pepper flakes until well blended. Pour over asparagus.

<u>Cover and chill for 8 hours.</u>

Drain before serving; arrange on a serving plate. Refrigerate any leftovers.

Note: this is really delicious and a great make-ahead company dish.

SIDES

CORN AND RICE CASSEROLE

Preheat oven to 350 degrees

2 cups of cooked rice
1 stick butter
1 large onion

2 cans cream corn
Salt and ground pepper to taste
2 Tbsp. sugar
1 small jar pimentos
1 egg
1/2 cup grated parmesan cheese

In large skillet, melt butter. Sauté onion until it looks clear. Add cream corn, salt and pepper, sugar and pimentos. Mix in cooked rice. Add beaten egg and mix together. Pour into 13x9 baking dish; sprinkle with parmesan cheese. Bake for 30 minutes; serve warm. Makes about 6 servings.

Notes:

This is a good side dish to serve with almost any entree. Sometimes I use a small can of green chilies instead of the pimentos. You could add chopped ham, chicken or bay shrimp to make it a one-dish entree for a luncheon...just serve with a tossed green salad or a colorful fruit salad and you're good to go!

SIDES

Notes:

SIDES

WHIPPED SWEET POTATOES

2 lbs. fresh sweet potatoes, baked and peeled
1 cup sour cream, divided
1/4 cup milk
1 egg
2 Tbsp. brown sugar, packed
1/2 tsp. ground cinnamon
Salt to taste
1 Tbsp. walnuts, finely chopped

Using electric mixer, whip baked sweet potatoes, 3/4 cup sour cream, milk, egg, sugar and cinnamon. Add salt to taste. Pour mixture into a 1-1/2 qt. casserole or into 6 individual ramekins. Microwave on medium-high 5-6 minutes or until thoroughly heated. Spread remaining 1/4 cup sour cream over top and sprinkle with walnuts. Microwave on medium-high 1 minute.

NOTES:

Another recipe that is good with a lot of different entrees... especially for holiday meals. It's a good alternative to the more typical ways to serve sweet potatoes. It is light and creamy and everyone seems to enjoy it.

If you prefer, you can substitute 1 (40oz.) can of sweet potatoes for the fresh ones.

SIDES

SWEET POTATO CASSEROLE

Preheat oven to 350 degrees

2 -1/2 lbs. sweet potatoes, peeled and cut into 2" cubes
2 large eggs
1 Tbsp. canola oil
1 Tbsp. honey
1/2 cup milk (I use 1%)
2 tsp. freshly grated orange zest
1 tsp. vanilla
1/2 tsp. salt (or to taste)
Topping:
1/2 cup whole-wheat flour
1/3 cup packed light brown sugar
4 tsp. frozen orange juice concentrate
1 Tbsp. canola oil
1 Tbsp. butter, melted
1/2 cup pecans, chopped

Place sweet potatoes in a large saucepan; cover with lightly salted water and bring to a boil. Cover and cook over medium heat until tender, 10-15 minutes. Drain well, return to the pan and mash.
Coat an 8" baking dish with cooking spray. Whisk eggs, oil and honey in a medium bowl. Add mashed sweet potatoes and mix well. Stir in milk, orange zest, vanilla and salt. Spread mixture in prepared baking dish.

Mix topping ingredients in a small bowl. Blend until crumbly. Sprinkle over the potato mixture. Bake for 35-45 minutes until top is lightly browned. To make ahead; prepare, cover and refrigerate for up to two days before baking. This is almost like a dessert!

SIDES

BAKED SQUASH

Preheat oven to 350 degrees

5 lb. medium-size yellow squash
2 eggs, beaten
1 cup bread crumbs, plus additional for topping
1 stick butter or margarine, cut into pieces
1/4 cup sugar
Salt and pepper to taste
2 Tbsp. onion, chopped
1 Tbsp. pimientos

Cut tips off squash and cut each squash into 3-4 pieces. Drop squash pieces into a large saucepan with enough boiling water to cover. Return to boil, reduce heat and cook until squash is tender. Drain in colander and mash with a fork. Combine mashed squash with the eggs, 1 cup bread crumbs, butter, sugar, salt and pepper, onion and pimientos. Turn into a 3 quart casserole that has been lightly greased or sprayed. Cover with a light layer of bread crumbs. Bake for 20-25 minutes or until lightly browned. Serves 10.
This is another great side dish and good way to use some of that garden bounty. I've never tried it with zucchini instead of the yellow squash or perhaps half of each, but I don't know why it wouldn't work.

You can easily half this recipe...or double it for a crowd.

The pimientos are really just for color so you don't have to add them. You could also add chopped ripe olives (1/4 cup) or jalapeno/serrano peppers for a little heat (1-2 finely chopped).

SIDES

TEX-MEX SUMMER SQUASH CASSEROLE

Preheat oven to 400 degrees

7 medium yellow summer squash, sliced (~10 cups)
  (zucchini works well instead, or combine the two)
2-1/4 cups (9 oz.) Cheddar cheese, shredded - DIVIDED
1 medium onion, chopped
1 can (4 oz.) green chilies, chopped
1 can (4 oz.) jalapeno peppers, drained and chopped
1/4 all-purpose flour
1/2 tsp. salt
3/4 cup salsa
4 green onions, sliced
1/4 cup red onion, chopped

In a large bowl, combine squash, 3/4 cup cheese, onion, green chilies and jalapenos. Sprinkle with flour and salt; toss to combine.

Transfer to a greased 13" x 9" baking dish. Bake, covered, 30-40 minutes or until squash is tender

Spoon salsa over top; sprinkle with remaining 1-1/2 cups cheese. Bake, uncovered, 10-15 minutes longer or until golden brown. Let stand 10 minutes. Top with green and red onions before serving.

Yield: 8-10 servings

SIDES

CURRIED SWEET POTATO PANCAKES

1-1/2 lbs. sweet potatoes, peeled and shredded
I small onion, grated
1/2 cup raisins or dried cranberries
2/3 cup flour
3 eggs, beaten
2 tsp. curry powder
1 tsp. Kosher salt
2 Tbsp. olive oil

In a large bowl, stir together shredded sweet potatoes, onion, raisins or dried cranberries and flour. Combine eggs with curry powder and Kosher salt in a small bowl; add to potato mixture and mix with your hands.

Warm olive oil in a large skillet over medium-high heat. Drop 1/3 cupful of mixture into skillet and fry, pressing with a spatula to flatten, until golden brown, 2-3 minutes per side. Keep warm in a 200 degree oven until ready to serve. Serve with sour cream, if desired.

SIDES

VEGETABLE PANCAKES

Pick your favorite vegetable:

Carrot: 1 large, peeled and grated
Zucchini: 1 medium, grated (sprinkle with salt, let stand 30 minutes, squeeze dry)
Corn: kernels from 1 large ear
Beet: 1/2 medium, peel and grate

Your prepped vegetable
3 Tbsp. flour
1/2 cup Parmesan cheese, grated
1 Tbsp. onion, grated
1 pinch Kosher salt

1 large egg
1 Tbsp. olive oil

Stir together vegetable, flour, Parmesan cheese, onion and salt in a medium bowl. Warm olive oil in a large nonstick skillet over medium-high heat. When oil is hot, stir egg into vegetable mixture. Drop heaping spoonfuls of batter into pan. Flatten slightly with back of spoon and cook until golden brown, about 2 minutes per side.

makes 5-6 pancakes

SIDES

QUINOA FRITTERS

2 1/2 cups cooked quinoa
2 large eggs
1-2 Tbsp. canola oil

Add fresh herbs (basil, chives)
Nuts, dried fruits (optional)

Lightly beat eggs; mix with quinoa and whatever you want to put in. Chill mixture for about 30 minutes.

Use a 1/4 cup measure to mold and drop mixture into hot oil.

SIDES

CORN FRITTERS

Preheat oven to 300 degrees

3 large ears of corn
2 egg yolks
4 tsp. all-purpose flour
4 tsp. cornmeal
1 tsp. granulated sugar
1/2 tsp. salt
1/4 tsp. pepper
2 egg whites
3-4 Tbsp. canola oil

Cut the kernels from the cobs to measure 9 oz. corn (about 2 cups). Separate the yolks from 2 eggs. In a small mixing bowl, beat the egg yolks with an electric mixer on high speed for about 5 minutes, or until thick and lemon colored. Stir in the corn kernels, flour, cornmeal, sugar, salt and pepper.

Wash the beaters thoroughly. In a medium bowl, beat the egg whites on high speed till stiff peaks form (tips stand straight). Gently fold the egg whites into the corn mixture.

Heat 2 Tbsp. oil in a large skillet. Add the batter by rounded tablespoons. Fry the fritters, a few at a time, over medium heat for 5-6 minutes, turning once, until they are golden brown and crisp; add oil as necessary. Keep cooked fritters warm in oven until all are fried. Serve warm.

Yield: 20-24 fritters

SIDES

Notes:

DESSERTS

DESSERTS

ROBERT'S FAVORITE FUDGE

Our son wouldn't consider it Christmas if I didn't make a batch of this fudge for him! Now the twins have discovered how good it is so Dad has to share! (The twins just turned 21!! Where did all those years go?)

Have all ingredients out and ready to use; have chocolate morsels open, measured and ready to pour into sugar mixture immediately after it finishes cooking. Stir until smooth and glossy.

1 small jar marshmallow cream
3/4 cup granulated sugar
1 (5 oz.) can evaporated milk
1/4 cup butter
1/4 tsp. salt

Combine in large, heavy gauge saucepan. Bring to a boil, stirring constantly, over moderate heat. When the mixture has reached roll boil continue to boil for 5 minutes, stirring constantly. Remove from heat.

 Add:
1 (12 oz.) pkg. semisweet chocolate morsels
Stir until chocolate is melted and mixture is smooth.

 Stir in:
 cup chopped nuts (optional)
1 tsp. vanilla

Pour into a foil-lined, greased 8" square pan. Chill until firm. Cut into squares before it gets too hard.
Makes about 2 1/4 pounds.

DESSERTS

TOFFEE

Lisa Byerley   2001

1 cup sugar
1 cup butter (2 sticks)
3 Tbsp. water
1 tsp. vanilla
3 regular sized chocolate bars or 1 large (6 oz) bar
1/2 cup pecans, chopped

Stirring constantly, bring sugar, water and butter to a boil (300 degrees on a candy thermometer)
Remove from heat. Add vanilla and stir quickly.
Pour into a foil-lined, buttered 8" square pan. Shake pan to distribute evenly. Let sit for a couple of minutes and then place the chocolate bars on top. After a few minutes spread the chocolate to cover the toffee mixture in pan and sprinkle with chopped nuts.

When completely cool, lift foil out of the pan and break or cut toffee into irregular pieces.

Store in an airtight container in a cool place.

NOTES:

I have started using a large (6 oz) Symphony Bar...the one with almonds and toffee chips. Works great and it is soooo good!

DESSERTS

CHOCOLATE COVERED CHERRIES

1/4 cup plus 2 Tbsp. butter, softened
2-1/2 cups powdered sugar, sifted
1-1/2 tsp. milk
1/4 tsp. vanilla
About 42 maraschino cherries with stems
1 (12 oz.) pkg. semisweet chocolate morsels
1 Tbsp. vegetable oil

Beat butter until creamy; gradually add sugar, beating well. Blend in milk and vanilla. Chill mixture for 2 hours or until firm.

Drain cherries, and dry thoroughly on paper towels. Place bowl of sugar mixture in a container of ice to keep mixture chilled. Shape a small amount of sugar mixture around each cherry. Place cherries on a wax paper-lined baking sheet; chill 2 hours or until firm.

*Combine chocolate morsels and vegetable oil and heat in microwave. Holding each cherry by the stem, dip into chocolate until covered; drain. Place on a wax paper-lined baking sheet. Chill until firm. Store in a cool place. Makes 3 ½ doz.

DESSERTS

NOTES:

Because these have a fondant layer, you purists may not like them, and I've notice that chocolate covered cherry lovers usually are purists! However, if you want to try something a little different, these take some extra time and effort but they are worth it. Wrapped up in a pretty box, they make a great gift.

*When melting chocolate in a microwave, heat for 20 - 30 seconds and stir; repeat until melted

DESSERTS

GRANOLA CLUSTERS

Preheat oven to 325 degrees

1/2 cup peanut butter (creamy or chunky)
1/2 cup honey
1 Tbsp. maple syrup
1 tsp. olive oil

1-1/2 cups uncooked old-fashioned oats
1/2 cup almonds, toasted and coarsely chopped
1/2 cup sweetened dried cranberries or apricots
1/2 cup sunflower seeds (optional)
1/4 cup chia seeds (optional)
1/4 cup mini chocolate chips
1/4 tsp. ground cinnamon
Dash of salt

Line a rimmed baking sheet with parchment paper. Combine peanut butter, honey, syrup and oil in a small pan. Cook over low heat until melted and the mixture can be easily stirred together. Remove from heat and set aside.

In a deep bowl, combine the remaining ingredients. Toss well to mix. Pour peanut butter mixture over oat mixture. Using a <u>rubber spatula coated with cooking spray,</u> stir until everything is evenly coated. Drop by heaping tablespoons onto the prepared baking sheet. They can be placed very close together because they don't spread.

Bake 20-22 minutes or until golden and crisp. Set tray on wire rack to cool completely. Store in an air-tight container or tin for up to 4 days. After that they will begin to get soft. Makes 2 dozen

DESSERTS

TRAIL MIX CLUSTERS

These are good for the summer because they don't require the oven

2 cups (12 oz.) semisweet chocolate chips
1/2 cup unsalted sunflower seeds
1/2 cup salted pumpkin seeds or pepitas
1/2 cup cashews, lightly toasted and coarsely chopped
1/2 cup pecan, toasted and coarsely chopped
1/4 cup flaked coconut (optional)
1/4 cup dried apricots, finely chopped
1/4 cup dried cranberries
1/4 cup dried cherries or blueberries

In a large, microwave-safe bowl, melt the chocolate chips; stir until smooth. Stir in the remaining ingredients.

Drop by tablespoonfuls onto waxed paper-lined baking sheets. Refrigerate until firm. Store in the refrigerator.

Makes 4 dozen

DESSERTS

LEMONADE ICE CREAM DESSERT

Preheat oven to 375 degrees

1-1/2 cups all-purpose flour
3/4 cup packed brown sugar
3/4 cup cold butter, cubed
3/4 cup pecans, chopped

1/2 gallon vanilla ice cream, softened
1 can (12 oz) frozen lemonade concentrate, thawed

In a small bowl, combine flour and brown sugar; cut in butter until crumbly. Stir in pecans. Spread in a single layer into a greased 15x10x1 baking pan.

Bake 9-12 minutes or until golden brown, stirring once. Cool on a wire rack 10 minutes.

In a large bowl, beat ice cream and lemonade until blended. Sprinkle half of the crumbles into a greased 13x9 baking dish. Spread with ice cream mixture, sprinkle with remaining crumbles. Cover and freeze overnight. Remove from the freezer 15 minutes before serving.

Makes 12-15 servings

DESSERTS

STRAWBERRY COOL WHIP DESSERT

A great no-bake summer dessert

4 cups fresh strawberries
1 (14 oz.) can sweetened condensed milk
1/4 cup fresh lemon juice
1 (8 oz.) container whipped topping
12 chocolate sandwich cookies
1-1/2 Tbsp. butter, melted

Line an 8" x 4" loaf pan with aluminum foil
Mash 2 cups of the strawberries in a large bowl
Stir in condensed milk, lemon juice and 2 cups of the whipped topping

Pour this mixture into the lined loaf pan
Combine chocolate sandwich cookies and melted butter.
Top the strawberry mixture with the cookie mixture, pressing gently

Cover with aluminum foil and freeze for at least 6 hours.

When ready to serve, invert loaf pan onto a serving plate and remove foil. "Frost" the sides with remaining whipped topping and garnish with remaining strawberries. Let sit for about 10 minutes before cutting and serving.

About 8-10 servings depending on how you cut it

DESSERTS

CHOCOLATE TRUFFLES

1-1/2 packages semisweet chocolate baking squares
1 (8 oz.) pkg. cream cheese, softened
3 cups powdered sugar, sifted
1-1/2 tsp. vanilla (or orange) extract
1 (12 oz.) pkg. (2 cups) milk chocolate morsels
3 Tbsp. vegetable oil

Melt the semisweet baking chocolate in a large microwavable bowl on HIGH 2-3 minutes, or until almost melted, stirring after each minute. Remove from microwave and stir until completely melted. Set aside.

Beat softened cream cheese until smooth. Gradually add sifted powdered sugar, beating until well blended. Add melted chocolate and vanilla or orange extract; mix well. Refrigerate for 1 hour. Shape into 1" balls. Place on cookie sheet and put into freezer for 1 hour.

Melt milk chocolate morsels in microwave for 1-2 minutes; stir until melted and add vegetable oil. Take truffles from freezer and drop them into the chocolate mixture one at a time. Stir quickly and gently to coat; remove with fork, shaking off excess coating. Return to cookie sheets and refrigerate 10-15 minutes until firm. Keep refrigerated in an airtight container.

Makes about 5 doz.

DESSERTS

NOTES:

Make certain you get the semisweet chocolate and cream cheese mixture thoroughly beaten and as smooth as possible. This will make your truffles really creamy.

Finished truffles freeze well.

NOTE: I've recently made some yummy peanut butter cups and thought about adding the recipe to the cookbook but, frankly, they were a pain in the patoot to make and require equipment most people wouldn't have on hand. So I've decided to modify the recipe to make a variation on the truffles.

Replace the first four ingredients of the truffle recipe with:

1-1/2 cups creamy peanut butter
1/2 cup powdered sugar (sifted)
1/2 cup graham cracker crumbs

Place the peanut butter in a bowl over hot water to soften. Mix in powdered sugar and graham cracker crumbs. Roll the mixture into 1" balls, place on cookie sheets lined with wax paper or parchment paper and place in freezer for 15-20 minutes. Remove from freezer and coat with the chocolate/oil mixture as you do for the truffles. Follow remaining instructions for truffles.

DESSERTS

CAKE NOTES:

Over the years I made many different kinds of cakes for the Tea Room, to be served on our "tea plate". Everyone had their favorite. Here is a list of the cakes and their various additions. Bake following instructions on the cake mix box.

Start with a basic cake mix of any flavor. I use a yellow cake mix for most of the cakes I do. Unfortunately, I tend to cook using "a dash of this and a pinch of that" so it's difficult to give very accurate quantities.

Hopefully this will inspire you to try combinations of your own.

Many of the cakes are seasonal but all are standard favorites in the Tea Room.
When adding any flavoring, extract, etc. Be sure to decrease the total fluid measurement by the amount of the added flavoring.

When I do orange and lemon cakes I also add zest from the rinds and I stir it in by hand after I have everything mixed to avoid having to clean it out of the mixer beaters.

DESSERTS

ORANGE POPPY SEED CAKE

1 small pkg. of instant cheesecake pudding mix
Orange juice to replace about an eighth of the required liquid
zest of the orange (if you are using real oranges!)
A capful of orange extract (if you want a stronger orange flavor)
1 Tbsp. poppy seeds

LEMON POPPY SEED CAKE

1 small pkg. of instant lemon pudding mix
Lemon juice (fresh squeezed) to replace about an eighth of the required liquid
Zest of 1 lemon
A capful of lemon extract (for a stronger lemon flavor)
1 Tbsp. poppy seeds

LEMON BLUEBERRY CAKE

1 small pkg. of instant lemon pudding mix
A capful of lemon extract
About 1 cup of frozen blueberries

DESSERTS

LEMON WALNUT CAKE

1 small pkg. of instant lemon pudding mix
A capful of lemon extract
About 1/2 cup of chopped walnuts (or pecans, if you prefer)

CHOCOLATE RASPBERRY CAKE

1 small pkg. instant chocolate pudding mix (Devil's Food flavor works well)
 About 1/4 cup of Raspberry flavoring (we use the coffee flavorings available in almost all markets)

CHOCOLATE NUT CAKE

1 small pkg. instant chocolate pudding mix (any variety)
About 1/2 cup of chopped nuts (your choice)

NOTES:

Note: When using chips, candy, berries, etc. In a cake be sure to dredge them in a little of the dry cake mix so they won't all (hopefully) sink to the bottom of the cake. Use mini chips when you can.

DESSERTS

CHOCOLATE ORANGE CAKE
1 small pkg. instant chocolate pudding mix
Capful of orange extract (for a stronger orange flavor)
2 Tbsp. orange juice (fresh squeezed)
1 Tbsp. orange zest
(I cut up Orange Slice candy to put on top of chocolate icing)

REECE'S PEANUT BUTTER CAKE
1 small pkg. instant chocolate pudding mix
1/2 pkg. Reece's peanut butter chips
1/4 cup peanut butter (creamy)

ENGLISH TOFFEE CAKE

1 small pkg. instant cheesecake pudding mix
1/2 pkg. English toffee bits
1/4 cup of English Toffee flavoring

ITALIAN CREME CAKE

1 small pkg. instant coconut cream pudding mix
Capful of coconut extract (for a stronger coconut flavor)
1/4 cup shredded coconut
1/4 cup chopped walnuts

DESSERTS

APPLE SPICE CAKE

1 small pkg. instant French vanilla pudding mix
2 small tart apples, peeled and shredded
Combined spices to equal 1 Tbsp. (I use cinnamon, nutmeg, cloves and allspice.)

CANDY CANE CAKE

(a nice Christmas cake)
1 small pkg. instant chocolate fudge or devil's food pudding mix
Capful of peppermint extract
About 1/4 cup crushed peppermint candy

APRICOT CAKE

1 small pkg. instant French vanilla pudding mix
About 1/2 cup apricots (fresh or canned, well drained)
A tiny bit of the juice if you use canned fruit (not too much or the cake will sink)

TROPICAL FRUIT CAKE

1 small pkg. instant Vanilla pudding mix
1/4 to 1/2 cup mixed dried fruit, chopped
1/4 cup chopped nuts (optional)

DESSERTS

ALMOND POPPY SEED CAKE

1 small package of cheesecake pudding mix
1 Tbsp. Poppy seeds
Capful of almond extract
Unlike most of the other cakes, this one is served with whipped cream and fresh strawberries

PUMPKIN SPICE CAKE

1 small pkg. of instant Cheesecake or Vanilla pudding Mix
1 cup of canned pumpkin (pure or pie mix)
1 Tbsp. Pumpkin pie spice (or a little more, to taste)

NOTES:

For most of these cakes we make a cream cheese frosting. We vary the flavor to match the cake but the basic ingredients are:

1 – 8 oz. package Cream Cheese, softened
1 cup+ Powdered sugar, sifted

Adjust the amounts to get a spreadable consistency. Mix together until smooth and then a variety of flavorings can be added according to which cake you've made. For a chocolate frosting, I add cocoa and either a little chocolate syrup or vanilla, or perhaps a flavoring like Hazelnut or Irish Cream. Sprinkle chopped nuts on top if you wish. Use your imagination and have fun!

DESSERTS

CHOCOLATE BANANA CAKE

1 small pkg. instant chocolate or chocolate fudge pudding mix
1 large very ripe banana, mashed (way past anything you would want to eat!)
Capful of banana extract (optional)

CHOCOLATE CHOCOLATE CHIP CAKE

1 small pkg. instant chocolate or chocolate fudge pudding mix
1/2 bag mini chocolate morsels (less likely to sink than regular chocolate morsels)

CARROT CAKE

1 small pkg. instant cheesecake or vanilla pudding mix
1 medium carrot, shredded
1 Tbsp. brown sugar
1/2 tsp. ground cinnamon
3 Tbsp. canned crushed pineapple, well drained

MEXICAN CHOCOLATE CAKE

1 small pkg. instant chocolate pudding mix
1-1/2 tsp. Cinnamon

DESSERTS

Notes:

DESSERTS

CHOCOLATE CINNAMON CAKE

Preheat oven to 400 degrees

Sift together in large bowl:
2 cups sugar
2 cups flour

Put into saucepan:
1 stick of butter
1/2 cup solid vegetable shortening
4 Tbsp. cocoa
1 cup water
Bring to rapid boil. Pour over flour/sugar mixture and stir well.

Add:
1/2 cup buttermilk
2 eggs, slightly beaten
1 tsp. soda
1 tsp. cinnamon (I usually add more)
1 tsp. vanilla

Bake for 20 minutes in:
13x2 baking pan for cake
15x2 baking pan for brownies

DESSERTS

ICING

Make icing five minutes before cake is done:
1 stick butter
4 Tbsp. cocoa
6 Tbsp. milk
In medium saucepan, melt together and bring to boil. Remove from heat and add 2 cups of powdered sugar, 1 tsp. vanilla and 1 cup chopped nuts. Beat well and spread on warm cake.

DESSERTS

OATMEAL CAKE
                           Sue Kerr 2000

Preheat oven to 350 degrees

1-1/2 cup boiling water
1 cup minute oats
1-1/2 cup flour
1 tsp. baking soda
1 tsp. cinnamon
1/2 tsp. nutmeg
1/2 tsp. cloves
1/2 tsp. salt
1 cup brown sugar, packed
1 cup granulated sugar
2 eggs
1/2 cup vegetable oil

Mix oats and boiling water. Sift flour, soda, cinnamon, nutmeg, cloves and salt together; stir into oat mixture.

Stir in sugars, eggs and oil. Mix until well blended. Pour into a 9x13 baking dish and bake at 350 degrees for about 30 minutes.

1 cup nuts, chopped
1 cup coconut
1 cup of brown sugar, packed
1 cup evaporated milk
1 stick butter, melted
1 tsp. vanilla

Mix together and pour over warm cake

DESSERTS

PUMPKIN ROLL

Preheat oven to 375 degrees

3 eggs
1 cup sugar
2/3 cup pumpkin, canned, not pie mix
3/4 cup flour
1 tsp. baking powder
2 tsp. cinnamon
1/2 tsp. nutmeg
1 tsp. ground ginger

Beat eggs for 1 minute, gradually add sugar and beat 4 minutes. Add pumpkin. Combine sifted dry ingredients, beat 1 minute. Line a 10x15 jelly roll pan (or a cookie sheet with a 1" lip) with waxed paper and grease. Pour pumpkin mixture evenly into pan making sure to fill all corners. Bake at 375 degrees for 12 minutes. Remove from oven and immediately turn onto clean tea towel sprinkled with powdered sugar. Remove wax paper and roll cake and towel together from small end. Cool completely. When cool, unroll and spread with filling. Reroll, wrap in plastic wrap and refrigerate until ready to use. Cut into servings; makes 8 or more depending on how thick you cut the slices.

Filling:
8 ounces cream cheese, softened
4 tsp. butter, softened
1/2 tsp. vanilla
1 cup powdered sugar
Beat together for 2 minutes

DESSERTS

CHOCOLATE ROLL CAKE

If you've never made a cake roll, you should try it! People are always impressed and, honestly, they just aren't that hard to make.

Preheat oven to 375 degrees

4 eggs, separated, at room temperature
1 cup granulated sugar, divided
1 tsp. vanilla extract
1/2 cup flour
1/2 cup cocoa
1/2 tsp. baking powder
1/4 tsp. baking soda
Pinch of salt
1/2 cup water
Powdered sugar

Line 15x10x1 jelly roll pan with foil; generously grease foil. Set aside.
In large mixer bowl, beat egg whites until soft peaks form. Gradually add 1/2 cup sugar, beating until stiff peaks form; set aside. In small mixer bowl, on medium speed, beat egg yolks and vanilla 3 minutes. Gradually add remaining 1/2 cup sugar; continue beating 2 additional minutes. Stir together flour, cocoa, baking powder, baking soda and salt; beating on low speed of electric mixer, add to egg yolk mixture alternately with water just until batter is smooth. Gradually and gently, fold chocolate mixture into beaten egg whites until well blended.

Spread batter evenly in prepared pan. Bake 12-15 minutes or until top springs back when touched lightly.

DESSERTS

Immediately loosen cake from edges of pan; invert onto clean towel sprinkled with powdered sugar. Carefully peel off foil. Immediately roll cake and towel together starting from narrow end; place on wire rack to cool.

When completely cooled, carefully unroll cake and remove towel. Spread cake with filling; reroll cake. Refrigerate until ready to slice and serve.

Notes:

I use the same filling I make for the Pumpkin Roll Cake.

DESSERTS

APPLE CAKE
            Wyndie Turpen 1999

I've had lots of apple cake recipes in my years of collecting and trying recipes but this is by far the best one I've ever tried. Thank you, Wyndie!

Preheat oven to 325 degrees

1-1/2 cups vegetable oil
2 cups granulated sugar
3 cups flour
1 tsp. baking soda
1 tsp. salt
3 eggs, beaten
4 medium sized apples, grated (I use a firm, tart apple)
2 tsp. almond extract
1 cup chopped pecans

Mix all ingredients with a spoon in a large bowl (mixture will be thick). Pour into a floured 9x13 baking pan. Cook at 325 degrees for 45 to 60 minutes.

Sauce/Icing:
1 stick butter
1 cup brown sugar, packed
1 (5 0z.) can evaporated milk
1 tsp. vanilla

Melt butter in a saucepan, stir in sugar to dissolve. Add milk. Cook to 230 degrees on a candy thermometer (soft ball stage). Add vanilla. Cool and spread on warm cake. Sprinkle with additional nuts if desired.

DESSERTS

Notes:

DESSERTS

CARROT CAKE

Preheat oven to 350 degrees

2 tsp. baking soda
2 tsp. cinnamon
1 tsp. salt
2 cups flour
3 eggs, well beaten
2 cups granulated sugar
1-1/2 cups vegetable oil
2 cups carrots, shredded
1 cup crushed pineapple, well drained
1 cup nuts, chopped

In a large mixing bowl, sift together baking soda, cinnamon, salt and flour. In a separate bowl, cream eggs, sugar and oil together and add to flour mixture. Stir in shredded carrots, pineapple and nuts, if desired. Bake at 350 degrees for 40 minutes in a 9x13 ungreased baking pan

Buttermilk Icing:

10 minutes before cake is done, in large saucepan:
1 cup granulated sugar
1/2 cup buttermilk
1 tsp. vanilla
1/2½ tsp. baking soda

Boil for 5 minutes, after roll boil, stirring constantly. Cool slightly and pour over warm cake.

DESSERTS

Notes:

This recipe was given to me by a neighbor in California many years ago. I like the fact that it has a boiled icing that soaks into the cake and makes it extra moist. As much as I love cream cheese icings, this is a nice change.

You'll know the mixture has reached roll boil when stirring doesn't stop the boiling action.

DESSERTS

SPICY PEAR CAKE
                              Karen Duesman   2002

Preheat oven to 350 degrees

1 cup water
1 cup chopped dried pears
2 cups flour
1-1/4 tsp. baking soda
1/2 tsp. salt
1 tsp. cinnamon
1 tsp. nutmeg (freshly grated)
1 tsp. cloves
1/2 cup vegetable oil
1 cup sugar
3 eggs
1 Tbsp. vanilla
1 cup chopped pecans

In saucepan, simmer pears and water. Sift together flour, baking soda, salt, cinnamon, nutmeg and cloves; set aside. In large mixing bowl, blend together oil, sugar, eggs and vanilla. Gradually add flour mixture and beat for about 3 minutes. Fold in drained pears and nuts. Pour into a Bundt pan or an angel food pan and bake about 45 minutes.

DESSERTS

ICING

1 stick butter
1 tsp. vanilla (Karen recommends a bit more)
1 tsp. orange or lemon zest, finely grated
3 cups powdered sugar, sifted
Orange or lemon juice, fresh squeezed; add by teaspoonful until icing is of spreading consistency

Notes:

Karen is an experienced baker and everything she has brought in to work for us to try has been terrific. This cake was such a winner we all begged her for the recipe which she graciously shared with us. She even brought us some dried pears! In the icing, Karen recommends lemon zest and orange juice. The alternatives are my addition. It's fun to experiment!

DESSERTS

BUTTER ALMOND CAKE

Preheat oven to 350 degrees

1/2 cup granulated sugar
1 tsp. vanilla extract
2/3 cup unsalted butter, plus small amount for pan
2 eggs
3/4 cup all-purpose flour
Glaze:
2 Tbsp milk
1 Tbsp flour
1/4 cup unsalted butter
1/3 cup blanched almonds, sliced
4 Tbsp granulated sugar

Melt 2/3 cup butter and allow to cool. Using an electric mixer, beat eggs, vanilla and sugar in large mixing bowl until light and fluffy. Add butter and flour to egg mixture and stir by hand.. Makes ~2 cups of batter.

Pour batter into an 8" greased and floured cake or tart pan. Bake for 25 minutes or until toothpick inserted in the center comes out clean.

In a saucepan, combine remaining 1/4 cup butter, 4 Tbsp. sugar, milk and flour. Bring to a boil and add almonds. Spread cake with glaze and bake for an additional 10 minutes, or until just beginning to turn light brown and crispy. Allow to cool on wire rack for 15 minutes before cutting. Serve warm or at room temperature.

Serves 8-10 (This is a dense, rich cake)

DESSERTS

ORANGE LEMON CAKE

Preheat oven to 350 degrees

1 cup (2 sticks) butter, melted
1 cup shredded coconut
4 eggs
3/4 cup granulated sugar
3/4 cup plus 1 Tbsp. slivered almonds
Zest of 1 lemon
Zest of 1 orange
1/2 cup freshly squeezed lemon juice
1/2 cup freshly squeezed orange juice
1 cup milk
1-1/2 cup all-purpose flour

Butter a 9" springform pan. Place the ingredients, working with half the batter at a time, in a food processor and mix until well combined, ~1 minute. Pour the mixture into the prepared cake pan.

Place the pan in the oven and bake for 1 hour, or until golden brown on top and a skewer inserted in the middle of the cake comes out clean. Remove from oven, cool in the pan on a wire rack, then turn out.

Yield: 8-10 pieces (this is a dense, rich cake)

DESSERTS

PEANUT BUTTER PIE

1 (8 oz.) pkg. cream cheese
1/4 cup crunchy peanut butter
1/2 cup sugar
1 tsp. vanilla
1 tub extra-creamy whipped topping, thawed

Soften cream cheese, blend in sugar, vanilla, and peanut butter. Fold in half of the whipped topping, then fold in the rest. Carefully place mixture in the crust (this is a sticky mixture and tends to pull the crust apart). Refrigerate overnight or freeze for later serving.

DESSERTS

ROOT BEER FLOAT PIE

1 carton (8 oz) whipped topping, thawed...DIVIDED
3/4 cup cold root beer
1/2 cup milk
1 small package instant vanilla pudding mix
1 (9") graham cracker crust

Set aside and refrigerate 1/2 cup whipped topping for garnish. In a large bowl, whisk the root beer, milk and pudding mix for 2 minutes. Fold in half of the whipped topping. Spread into graham cracker crust.

Spread remaining whipped topping over pie. Refrigerate for at least 8 hours or overnight.

Dollop reserved whipped topping over each serving; top with maraschino cherry if desired.

Yield: 8 servings

DESSERTS

FAMILY RECIPES:

When we first started the Tea Room, we asked relatives what their favorite recipes were. We had a good response, but one of the perennial favorites has been this simple recipe supplied by Paul's mother's sister. Also known as the 'Eagle Brand Lemon Pie'.

Both versions of the lemon pie freeze very well. Just remove to the refrigerator for a couple of hours before serving.

AUNT PEARL'S LEMON PIE

Juice from 2 lemons
Zest from 2 lemons
1 (8 oz) package cream cheese, softened
1 can sweetened condensed milk
1 graham cracker crust

Put condensed milk in food processor. Add lemon zest and start processor on low. Slowly add cream cheese in chunks; process until smooth. Add lemon juice and process until thoroughly mixed. Pour into crust and store overnight in the refrigerator. Pie can also be frozen for later use.

LOW-FAT LEMON PIE

For this variation on the lemon pie recipe, substitute no fat cream cheese and no fat sweetened condensed milk. For a further reduction, use a reduced fat graham cracker crust. The only fat in this recipe is in the crust, so you could make a zero fat recipe by serving the mixture in a dessert dish without the crust.

DESSERTS

Notes:

DESSERTS

CINNAMON APPLE CREPES

Crepe:
1 cup baking mix (like Bisquick)
2 Tbsp. sugar
1 cup water
2 eggs, beaten

In a small bowl, whisk together all ingredients until smooth.
Cover and chill for at least 1 hour.
Heat crepe pan (or shallow 8" skillet) to just above medium high heat. Grease with vegetable oil spray. Pour about 2 Tbsp. batter into hot pan and immediately tilt pan until batter covers the bottom. Cook until edges start to dry and center is set. Turn crepe to brown slightly on other side (about 30 seconds).

Filling:
1 can of apple pie filling
2 Tbsp. butter, melted
1 Tbsp. powdered cinnamon
Cut the apples into smaller pieces, if necessary (varies by brand).
Stir in the butter and cinnamon. Mix equal parts of powdered cinnamon and sugar and put in a salt shaker.

Place a crepe on a small plate. Spread 1/4 cup of the filling down the middle of the crepe and fold both sides over. Heat in the microwave on high for about 1 minute. Put whipped cream on top and dust with the sugar/cinnamon mixture.

DESSERTS

NOTES ON CREPES:

We made our own cinnamon crepes. Commercial crepes are okay to substitute, but the flavor of the cinnamon in the crepe definitely makes a difference.

This recipe will make 10-12 crepes. Use the following method to freeze the unfilled crepes for future use: As you make each crepe, put it on a piece of wax paper to cool. When all of the crepes are cool you can stack them with the wax paper layers in between each one. Put the finished stack into a plastic freezer bag. To use: remove desired number of crepes from freezer; microwave each one for a few seconds to thaw and warm.

If you want to use a savory filling in your crepes simply leave out the cinnamon.

DESSERTS

FROZEN CAPPUCCINOS

The easiest way to make a frozen cappuccino is to start with a prepared mix. We have developed our own, consisting of:

1/2 cup cocoa
1 cup sugar
1/2 cup thickener (*a commercial product)

Blend together and store in a plastic container with a coffee measure.

To make the frozen drink, into a blender put:

1 shot of espresso
1-1/2 coffee measures of your mix
1/2 oz. half and half (use skim for less fat)

Mix thoroughly on low

Turn off blender and add either ice or ice cream. Blend first on low speed to get rid of the big chunks and slowly increase speed until mixture is smooth. The amount of ice or ice cream will depend on the temperature of the coffee and the ice or ice cream. Try starting with about a cup.

If you don't have an espresso machine, you can make a suitable substitute with 1 oz. of hot water and one coffee measure of instant coffee.

*The purpose of the thickener is to keep the finished product from separating and is not essential.

DESSERTS

PRALINE CRUMB CARAMEL CHEESECAKE BARS

Preheat oven to 350 degrees

Cookie base and topping:
1 pouch (1 lb. 1.5 oz) sugar cookie mix
1/2 cup cold butter
1/2 cup pecans, chopped
1/2 cup toffee bits

Filling:
2-8 oz. packages cream cheese, softened
1/2 cup sugar
2 Tbsp. flour
1/2 cup caramel topping, divided
1 tsp. vanilla
1 egg

Place cookie mix in bowl and cut in butter until mixture is crumbly. Reserve 1-1/2 cups for topping. Press remaining mixture into a 13x9 baking pan that has been greased with cooking spray. Bake for 10 minutes.

In a large bowl, beat cream cheese, sugar, flour, 1/4 cup of the caramel topping, vanilla and egg with electric mixer on medium speed until smooth. Spread cream cheese mixture evenly over partially baked cookie base. Sprinkle with reserved crumb topping, pecans and toffee bits. Bake 35-40 minutes or until light golden brown. Cool 30 minutes. Refrigerate for about 2 hours until chilled. Drizzle with remaining caramel topping.

For bars, cut into 9 rows by 4 rows. Store covered in refrigerator. Makes 36 bars.

DESSERTS

ICEBOX BANANA PUDDING

1 large package of vanilla instant pudding
12 oz. container of whipped topping
1 large can sweetened-condensed milk
1 box of vanilla wafers
Bananas

Prepare pudding as directed; chill in refrigerator until set. Mix in whipped topping and sweetened-condensed milk. Spread a small amount in the bottom of a serving dish. Line bottom and sides of dish with vanilla wafers. Slice bananas and distribute evenly over the vanilla wafers. Sprinkle bananas with a little fresh lemon juice to keep them from turning brown. Spread more pudding mixture over the bananas. Repeat until all the ingredients are used.

Sprinkle vanilla wafer crumbs over top of dish. Make a few hours before using and chill, covered, in the refrigerator.

DESSERTS

FORGOTTEN COOKIES

Preheat oven to 350 degrees (ESSENTIAL)

2 egg whites, at room temperature
2/3 cup sugar
1 cup chocolate chips
1 cup chopped nuts
1 tsp. vanilla extract

Beat eggs until foamy. Add sugar 1 Tbsp. at a time, beating after every addition. Beat until egg whites are stiff. Fold in chocolate chips and nuts. Add vanilla.

Drop onto cookie sheet that has been lined with foil. Have oven PREHEATED to 350 degrees. Place cookie sheet on center shelf in oven. Turn off heat. DO NOT OPEN oven door for 12 hours.

Makes 2 doz.

NOTES:

I put these in to "cook" before I go to bed and they are ready the next morning. Try these when the weather is dry; they don't turn out well when the air is humid.

DESSERTS

PEANUT BUTTER COOKIES

This recipe was provided by Paul's mother, Pauline Harrison. It has been a family favorite for years.

Preheat oven to 350 degrees

I pkg. chocolate kisses
1 cup crunchy peanut butter
1 Crisco stick (butter flavor)
1 tsp. vanilla
2 eggs
1 cup brown sugar (packed)
1 cup granulated sugar
3 cups flour
1/2 tsp. salt
2 tsp. baking soda

Cream together Crisco stick, vanilla, eggs, brown sugar and granulated sugar. Sift together flour, salt and baking soda. Add flour mixture to the sugar mixture and blend well. Stir in the crunchy peanut butter. Shape into balls and roll in sugar. Bake on greased cookie sheet at 350 degrees for 15-18 minutes. Put chocolate kiss in the center of warm cookie and press in slightly. Leave cookies on baking sheet for a few minutes to set and then remove to a rack to cool.

Have all the chocolate kisses unwrapped and ready to use before starting cookies.

We have always made super-sized cookies but you can make them any size you want. Recipe makes 18 very large or about 3-4 dozen regular sized cookies.

DESSERTS

Mom always used creamy peanut butter in her cookies but we like to use the crunchy variety.

Marlene (who made the ones at the Tea Room) liked to add a couple of tablespoons of milk to make the mixture a little creamier.

DESSERTS

VIENNA SUGAR COOKIE

Preheat oven to 375 degrees

1 pkg. day yeast (1/4 ounce)
3 Tbsp. lukewarm water
2 sticks of butter, unsalted
2 cups flour, sifted
1 cup sugar

Dissolve yeast in lukewarm water. Cream butter, adding flour gradually. Stir yeast into flour mixture and blend well. Chill for an hour or two.

Put 1 cup sugar on waxed paper. Pinch off pieces of dough the size of small walnuts Shape into balls. Press flat into sugar until thin. Keep flipping each ball of dough over until it's the size of a flat doughnut. Bake on ungreased cookie sheet at 375o for 8 to 12 minutes or until very lightly browned. Makes about 30 3" rounds.

NOTES:

These cookies have a delicate lacey look and are nice to serve with coffee or tea.

DESSERTS

CHOCOLATE CHIP SHORTBREAD COOKIE

Preheat oven to 350

2 cups butter, softened
2 cups powdered sugar
2 tsp. vanilla
4- 1/2 cups flour
1 (12oz) package of mini chocolate chips

Cream butter, sugar and vanilla together. Gradually add flour and then the chocolate chips. Roll into logs and chill. Cut about 1/4" thick and bake on parchment paper lined baking sheets. Bake for 11 minutes. Cool on racks.

Makes 90 small cookies. Store in airtight container.

DESSERTS

CHOCOLATE BISCOTTI

Preheat oven to 350

4 oz. of semisweet or dark chocolate chips
1 stick butter
2 eggs
1 cup sugar
1 tsp. vanilla
2 to 2-1/4 cups flour
1/2 cup unsweetened cocoa powder
1-1/2 tsp. baking powder (make sure it's fresh!)
1 tsp. salt
1 beaten egg white for glaze (optional)

Melt butter and chocolate together in microwave for about 1-1/2 minutes on high. Set aside.

Beat the eggs and sugar until lightened; about 2 minutes using an electric hand mixer. Add vanilla and chocolate mixture.

Stir together 2 cups of flour, cocoa, baking powder and salt. Stir in the chocolate mixture until just combined. (You should have a soft, but not sticky, dough. Add the extra 1/4 cup flour if dough is too sticky.)

Divide the dough in half on a large cookie sheet and form into logs that are about 3 1/2" by 9". Brush logs with egg white if desired.

Bake for 25 minutes until tops are set.

DESSERTS

Reduce oven to 275. Let the logs cool as long as possible; at least 30 minutes. The cooler they are the easier they are to cut. Carefully cut the logs in 1/2" thick slices. Arrange the slices on a baking sheet and bake for 20 minutes. Remove from oven. Carefully turn slices over and bake for another 20 minutes. Cool on a wire rack. Store in an airtight container.

Notes:

DESSERTS

TOFFEE COOKIES

Preheat oven to 350 degrees

1 cup unsalted butter (2 sticks)
1 cup brown sugar, packed
1 box Saltine crackers
2 cups milk chocolate morsels
1 cup pecans (or walnuts), finely chopped

Line 18"x12" cookie sheet with foil; grease lightly. Cover bottom of cookie sheet with a single layer of Saltine crackers. Bring butter and sugar to a rolling boil; continue boiling for 3 minutes, stirring constantly. Pour over Saltine crackers and bake at 350 degrees for 5 minutes. Sprinkle milk chocolate morsels over Saltines and spread quickly to cover. Sprinkle nuts evenly over the top and let set until cold. Cut into squares or rectangles with a pizza wheel or sharp knife; may also be broken into pieces like toffee.

Notes:

DESSERTS

PUMPKIN ORANGE COOKIES

Preheat oven to 375 degrees

2-1/2 cups flour
1/2 tsp. baking soda
1/2 tsp. salt
1 cup (2 sticks) unsalted butter, softened
1 cup granulated sugar
1/2 cup brown sugar, packed
1 egg
1 (15 oz.) can pumpkin (not pie mix)
2 Tbsp. orange juice, fresh squeezed
1 tsp. orange zest
1/2 cup chopped nuts (optional)

Combine dry ingredients in medium bowl. Combine butter and both sugars in large mixer bowl; beat until creamy. Add egg, pumpkin, orange juice, and orange peel; beat until combined. Gradually add flour mixture; beat until thoroughly combined. Stir in nuts. Drop dough by rounded Tbsp. on to ungreased cookie sheets. Bake at 375 degrees for 12-14 minutes or until edges are set. Remove to wire rack to cool. Spread each cookie with about 1/2 tsp. orange glaze. Makes 4 1/2-5 dozen.

Orange Glaze:
1-1/2 cups sifted powdered sugar
2-3 Tbsp. orange juice, fresh squeezed
1/2 tsp. orange zest

Combine until smooth.

DESSERTS

DROP SUGAR COOKIES

Preheat oven to 350 degrees

1 cup butter, softened
1-1/2 cups powdered sugar, sifted
1 cup granulated sugar
1 cup vegetable oil
2 eggs, beaten
1 tsp. vanilla
4 cups flour
1 tsp. cream of tartar (make sure it's fresh)
1/2 tsp. salt
1 tsp. baking soda
1-2 Tbsp. lemon zest (optional)

Sift flour, salt, baking soda and cream of tartar together. Mix with remaining ingredients in large bowl until well blended. Drop by teaspoonful onto cookie sheet about 2" apart. Sprinkle with granulated sugar. Bake at 350 degrees for 10-11 minutes or until brown on edges. Makes about 5 dozen.

NOTES:

It's unusual to find a recipe for sugar cookies that is dropped instead of shaped. It's faster and easier and they really taste good.

DESSERTS

HAYSTACKS

2 cups Chinese Chow Mein noodles
1 cup peanuts, lightly salted
1 (12 oz.) pkg. of either chocolate or butterscotch morsels

Melt morsels in microwave; mix with Chow Mien noodles and peanuts. Drop by teaspoonful onto wax paper-lined cookie sheet to cool. Makes about 3 dozen.

This is a fun, easy recipe that kids enjoy making…and eating!! For Christmas, try using white chocolate and chopped green and red candied cherries.

DESSERTS

MACAROONS

Preheat oven to 350 degrees

1 cup almond paste
1 cup sugar
1 tsp. orange zest
Pinch of salt
2 egg whites, beaten stiff

Blend almond paste, sugar, orange peel and salt by working with hands. Fold in egg whites. Drop by tsp. onto lightly greased cookie sheet. Bake in 350 degree oven 15-17 minutes or until light golden brown. Cool slightly, transfer to rack to cool completely. Makes about 30.

Variations: Drop by tsp. into 1 cup toasted chopped almonds. Coat evenly. Bake as above. Lightly press 1 whole almond into each macaroon before baking.

Yield: ~ 2 dozen

DESSERTS

CHOCOLATE CAKE MIX COOKIES

Preheat oven to 350 degrees

1 (18.5 oz.) package cake mix (I use Chocolate Fudge or Devil's Food)
1/2 cup butter, softened
2 large eggs
1/4 cup brown sugar, firmly packed
1 tsp. vanilla extract
1 cup semi-sweet chocolate chips
1/2 cup pecans or walnuts, chopped (optional)

Place cake mix, eggs, butter, brown sugar and vanilla extract in large bowl. Stir with spoon until thoroughly blended. Stir in chocolate chips and nuts, if using. Drop by level tablespoonfuls onto parchment paper lined baking sheets.

Bake for 12 minutes for chewy cookies, 14 minutes for crisp cookies. Cool for a few minutes on baking sheets. Remove to cooling racks. Cool completely. Store in airtight container.

Yield: ~ 2 dozen

DESSERTS

LEMON CAKE MIX COOKIES

Preheat oven to 350 degrees

1 (18.5 oz.) lemon supreme cake mix
1 Tbsp. freshly squeezed lemon juice
1/3 cup canola oil
2 eggs, lightly beaten

Glaze:
1 cup powdered sugar, sifted
2 Tbsp. freshly squeezed lemon juice

Combine first 4 ingredients and roll into 1" balls. Drop onto parchment paper lined baking sheets. Bake 8 minutes...do not over bake! Let rest on baking sheets for a few minutes before transferring to wire racks to cool.

Combine sifted powdered sugar and lemon juice to make a glaze. Glaze cookies after they are completely cooled.

Yield: 4 dozen

DESSERTS

LEMON SNOWDROP SHORTBREAD COOKIES

Preheat oven to 325 degrees

1 cup unsalted butter, room temperature
2/3 cup confectioners sugar, sifted
2-1/2 tsp. lemon zest
2 tsp. freshly squeezed lemon juice
pinch of salt
2-2/3 cups all-purpose flour

For Rolling:
1 cup confectioners sugar, sifted

Beat the butter and sugar together with a spoon or electric mixer until creamy. Add the lemon zest, lemon juice and salt; mix until combined. Add the flour; mix until well blended. Shape the dough in 1" balls and set them 1" apart on parchment paper-lined baking sheets.

Bake until cookies are light golden and give slightly when pressed; 18-20 minutes. Let the cookies cool slightly on the baking sheet. While they are still warm, roll them in sifted confectioners sugar. Transfer to wire rack to cool.

Yield: 3 dozen

DESSERTS

CHOCOLATE CHIP OATMEAL COOKIES

Preheat oven to 375 degrees

1 cup unsalted butter, softened
3/4 cup granulated sugar
3/4 cup light brown sugar, firmly packed
2 eggs
1 tsp. vanilla extract
3 cups quick-cooking oats
1-1/2 cups all-purpose flour
1 package (3.4 oz.) instant vanilla pudding mix
1 tsp. baking soda
1 tsp. salt
2 cups (12 oz.) semisweet chocolate chips
1 cup nuts, chopped (optional)
1/2 cup dried cranberries (optional)

In a large bowl, cream butter and sugars until light and fluffy. Beat in eggs and vanilla.. Combine the oats, flour, dry pudding mix, baking soda and salt; gradually add to creamed mixture and blend well. Stir in chocolate chips. Add nuts and/or dried cranberries, if using.

Drop by rounded teaspoonfuls 2" apart onto parchment paper-lined baking sheets. Bake for 10-12 minutes or until lightly browned. Let cool slightly and transfer to wire racks.

Yield: ~7 dozen

You can substitute instant chocolate pudding mix for the vanilla if you like.

DESSERTS

LEMON OATMEAL SUGAR COOKIES

(this batter must be refrigerated, covered, for about 2 hours or until firm enough to shape)

Preheat oven to 375 degrees

1 cup unsalted butter, softened
2 cups sugar
2 eggs
2 tsp. lemon zest
3 Tbsp freshly squeezed lemon juice
2-3/4 cups all-purpose flour
1 cup quick-cooking oats
2 tsp. baking powder
1/4 tsp. salt
Additional sugar for stamping

In a large bowl, cream butter and sugar until light and fluffy. Beat in eggs, lemon zest and lemon juice. In another bowl, whisk flour, oats, baking powder and salt; gradually beat into creamed mixture.

Shape level tablespoons of dough into balls; place 2" apart on parchment paper-lined baking sheets. Coat bottom of a glass with cooking spray, then dip in sugar. Press cookies with bottom of glass to flatten, redipping in sugar as needed. Bake 10-11 minutes or until edges are light brown. Remove from baking sheets to wire racks to cool

Yield: 6 dozen

DESSERTS

PEANUT BUTTER SNOWBALL COOKIES

1/2 cup peanut butter
2 Tbsp. unsalted butter, softened
1 cup powdered sugar, sifted
8 oz. white candy coating, chopped

In a bowl, stir together peanut butter and butter. Gradually add sifted powdered sugar, stirring until well combined. Shape mixture into 1" balls and place on wax paper. Let stand 20 minutes or until dry.

In a saucepan, cook and stir candy coating over low heat until melted and smooth. Cool slightly. Dip balls, one at a time into coating, using toothpick or fork. Allow excess coating to drip off.

Place coated balls on wax paper; let stand until firm. Store in an air-tight container in refrigerator.

Yield: 30 cookies

DESSERTS

PRETZEL BITES

Preheat oven to 350 degrees

1 (8 oz) bag small square pretzels
2 (14 oz) bags Hershey's Hugs or Kisses
1 (13 oz) bag M&Ms plain chocolate candy

Spread pretzels out on a baking sheet. Unwrap hugs (or Kisses) and place one on top of each pretzel. Place in oven for ~3 minutes. Watch them carefully! The shape of the candy should remain but it should be soft when you press on it.

Remove from oven and immediately press one M&M on top, pushing down to spread out the chocolate.
Chill and store in an air-tight container. For Christmas, I get red and green M&Ms. At Easter you could use pastels. I've actually picked all the red and blue colors out of a package of M&Ms when I made them for the 4th of July.

Fun and delicious!

Yield: 1 large baking sheet full, ~8 dozen

DESSERTS

NO BAKE CHOCOLATE COOKIES

1-1/2 cups sugar
1/2 cup milk
1/3 cup unsweetened cocoa powder
1/2 cup unsalted butter
3 cups quick-cooking oats
1 tsp. vanilla extract
1/4 tsp. salt
1/2 cup peanut butter (optional)

Line baking sheets with parchment paper. Combine sugar, milk, cocoa and butter in saucepan over medium-high heat. Bring to a boil and cook 3-4 minutes.

Stir in oats and vanilla (and peanut butter, if using) and stir vigorously until everything in combined and coated.

Drop by rounded tablespoonfuls onto paper line baking sheets. Let cool for 10-15 minutes. Refrigerate to speed cooling. Store in air-tight container in refrigerator for 7-10 days.

Yield: ~3 dozen

DESSERTS

CREAM CHEESE ALMOND BARS

Preheat oven to 350 degrees

Crust:
1 cup unsalted butter, cubed
1/2 cup powdered sugar, sifted
2 cups all-purpose flour
Filling:
1 (8 oz) package cream cheese, softened
1/2 cup granulated sugar
2 eggs
1 tsp. almond extract
Frosting:
1-1/2 cups powdered sugar, sifted
1-1/2 Tbsp. milk
1/4 cup butter, softened
1 tsp. almond extract
1/2 cups sliced almonds, toasted

Crust: cut butter into dry ingredients and pat into 9x13 pan. Bake for 20-25 minutes.

Filling: Mix sugar and cream cheese with electric mixer until well creamed. Beat in eggs and almond extract until fluffy. Pour over the crust while still hot. Bake for 15-20 minutes. Cool completely.

Frosting; Cream sugar and butter; add milk and almond extract and mix well. Spread evenly on baked, cooled filling Sprinkle toasted almonds on top. Store in refrigerator.

Yield: 24 bars

DESSERTS

FROSTED WALNUT BROWNIE CUPS

Preheat oven to 350 degrees

2 cups (12 oz) semisweet chocolate chips
1 cup butter, cubed
1-1/3 cups granulated sugar
4 eggs
2 tsp. vanilla extract
1 cup all-purpose flour
1 cup walnuts, chopped

Ganache:
2 cups (12 oz) semisweet chocolate chips
3/4 cup heavy whipping cream

In a microwave, melt chocolate chips and butter; whisk until smooth. Cool slightly.

In a large bowl, beat sugar and eggs. Stir in vanilla and chocolate mixture. Gradually add flour; stir in walnuts. Fill paper-lined miniature muffin cups almost full.

Bake for 20-23 minutes or until a toothpick inserted in the center comes out clean. Cool for 5 minutes before removing from pans to wire rack to cool completely.

Ganache: Place chocolate chips in a small bowl. In a small saucepan, bring cream just to a boil Pour over chocolate; whisk until smooth. Cool for 30 minutes or until ganache reaches a spreading consistency, stirring occasionally. Spread over brownies;

Yield: ~30

DESSERTS

Notes:

DESSERTS

BREAD PUDDING WITH LEMON SAUCE

                                                        Pat Roberts   1996

Preheat oven to 300 degrees

4 slices of bread, buttered and cubed
4 eggs, slightly beaten
1/4 cup sugar
2 cups milk
1/2 cup white raisins (optional)
2 Tbsp. butter, melted
1 tsp. vanilla extract

Cream eggs with sugar. Scald milk and add gradually to the egg/sugar mixture. Add bread cubes and raisins and blend well. Add melted butter and vanilla extract. Pour into buttered 2 quart baking dish. Set dish in pan of boiling water. Bake at 300 degrees for 1 hour or until tester comes out clean. Cool slightly and serve with Lemon Sauce.

DESSERTS

LEMON SAUCE

1/4 cup cold water
1 Tbsp. corn starch
1/2 cup sugar
Pinch of salt
3/4 cup boiling water
1 Tbsp. butter
2 Tbsp. lemon juice, fresh squeezed
1/2 tsp. lemon zest

In a 3 quart saucepan blend cold water, corn starch, sugar and salt. Stir in boiling water and cook for 1 minute until sauce is thickened and transparent. Add butter, lemon juice and lemon zest and mix well. Pour over bread pudding. Best served warm.

DESSERTS

This cheesecake recipe is not one we used for the Tea Room because the finished product doesn't freeze well. It will keep for several days in the refrigerator, however...if any is left!

If using a ready-made graham cracker crust use slightly less than one pint of sour cream. If making your own graham cracker crust, make it a deep dish to accommodate the entire amount of sour cream.

Try this easy crust recipe...

GRAHAM CRACKER CRUST

16 graham cracker squares
1/4 cup sugar (you can cut this down by half)
1/3 cup butter, melted
1/4 cup walnuts or pecans, finely chopped

Mix together well and press into a deep 9" pie pan.

DESSERTS

TWO-LAYER CHEESECAKE

Preheat oven to 350 degrees

Bottom layer:
1 (8 oz.) pkg. cream cheese
1/2 cup powdered sugar
3 eggs
1 tsp. lemon extract

Mix together in a food processor. Pour into graham cracker crust. Bake at 350 degrees for exactly 20 minutes.

Top layer:
1 pint sour cream (use slightly less if using a commercial crust)
3 Tbsp. granulated sugar
1/2 tsp. vanilla

Mix together and gently spoon over baked cream cheese layer. Bake for another 5-10 minutes.
Refrigerate for at least 16 hours before serving; the longer the better.

DESSERTS

DOUBLE CHOCOLATE BROWNIES

Preheat oven to 325 degrees

3/4 cup all purpose flour
1/4 tsp. baking soda
1/4 tsp. salt
3 Tbsp. butter
3/4 cup granulated sugar
1 Tbsp. water
1 (12 oz.) pkg. semisweet chocolate morsels, divided
1 tsp. vanilla
2 eggs
1/2 cup chopped nuts (optional)

Sift flour, baking soda and salt together; set aside. Place butter, sugar and water in saucepan and bring just to a boil. Remove from heat. Add half (1 cup) chocolate morsels and vanilla. Stir until chocolate melts and mixture is smooth. Add eggs, one at a time, beating well after each addition. Gradually blend in flour mixture. Stir in remaining 1 cup of chocolate morsels and nuts. Spread into greased 9" square pan.

Bake at 325 degrees for about 30 minutes. Cool completely. Cut into 16 2-1/4 " squares. Very fudgy!

NOTES:

If you like your brownies really fudgy instead of cake-like, this is a good recipe to try.

DESSERTS

Notes:

TEA TIME TREATS

TEA TIME TREATS

SPECIAL CHICKEN SANDWICH

1 lb. cooked white meat chicken
1 cup pecans
1 cup dates
10 rashers of bacon (medium thickness, cooked till crisp)
1/2 cup mayo

Chop chicken in a food processor. Add pecans and dates and continue chopping. Add mayo and process until of spreadable consistency. You may have to add more mayo if not used when made as it tends to thicken when refrigerated.

NOTES:

So many of the recipes in this book were done for teas but they all seem to fit into other headings. These recipes are very special and unique to Cinnamon Sticks.

This may sound like a strange combination of ingredients, but I've never found anyone who doesn't love these sandwiches. We used mini croissants when we made them for teas...very elegant, very yummy.

TEA TIME TREATS

CUCUMBER SANDWICH

1 loaf thin sandwich bread or hoagie rolls
1 cucumber, sliced VERY thin
1 (8 oz.) pkg. cream cheese, softened
1 Tbsp. fresh chives, chopped
1 tsp. lemon juice, fresh squeezed (optional)

Cut bread into 2" rounds with a biscuit cutter or make ¼ inch slices in the rolls. Mix together cream cheese, chives and lemon juice if desired. Spread on rounds of bread and top with a slice of cucumber.
The Brits put a thin layer of butter on the bread before the cream cheese layer to keep the bread from getting soggy. We just like to make them and serve them before that happens. If you need to make them ahead; place them on a platter in a single layer, cover with a slightly damp paper towel and then wrap with plastic wrap and refrigerate.

These are such an English Tea tradition that we really must include them...besides, they're Sarah Sutter's favorite sandwich. Sarah worked for us part-time while she went to UNT. She is now a career woman, working for an American company in Wiesbaden, Germany. We miss her!!

TEA TIME TREATS

ORANGE CURRANT SCONES

Preheat oven to 350 degrees
Zest from 1 orange
Juice from 1 orange
1/4 cup currants
4 cups self-rising flour
1/2 cup sugar
1 tsp. salt
1 stick unsalted butter, cold
1/3 cup milk
2 eggs

In a small bowl, combine orange juice, zest and currants; set aside. Place flour, sugar and salt in bowl; cut small cubes of cold butter into flour mixture with pastry cutter. Stir in milk and eggs. Add orange juice/currant mixture and blend well. Knead dough until all the dry ingredients are incorporated and the dough is smooth. Mound dough to cover a dinner plate and cut into 8 wedges. Allow to rise in refrigerator. Scones can then be separated and baked or frozen for future use. If frozen, place unthawed on cookie sheet and bake in 350 degree oven for 25-30 minutes or until golden brown.

DEVONSHIRE CREAM

1 (8 oz.) pkg. of cream cheese, softened
1 cup sour cream
1/2 tsp. almond extract
1 cup powdered sugar, sifted

TEA TIME TREATS

Notes:

Orange Currant scones are what we always made in the Tea Room but there are many variations that can be used. Just replace the orange juice with more milk and add anything you would like: nuts, mini chocolate morsels, dried fruits are only a few suggestions. Try savory scones sometime...replace the orange juice, orange zest and currants with 1/2 cup of shredded cheese and your favorite herbs.

We will always think of these as Marlene's scones because no one made them as well as she did. Marlene Reaves was part of the Tea Room for many years and she did most of the baking...the wonderful Peanut Butter Cookies were always made by her. Some people just have that magic touch!

Serve your sweet scones with butter or Devonshire Cream and strawberry jam. Yum!

OK, you've asked for it, so here it is. Peggy's very own original Devonshire Cream recipe. Be advised, this is not REAL Devonshire Cream, just a recipe we find scrumptious with scones. Just mix the ingredients together in the order listed until creamy - enjoy!!

TEA TIME TREATS

LEMON SQUARES

Margie Papillard 1989

Preheat oven to 350 degrees

Crust:
1 cup flour
1/4 cup powdered sugar
1/2 cup butter, cold, cubed

Filling:
2 eggs
3/4 cup granulated sugar
3 Tbsp. lemon juice, fresh squeezed
1 Tbsp. lemon zest
2 Tbsp. flour
1/2 tsp. baking powder

Sift together flour and powdered sugar. Cut in butter until mixture clings together. Pat into ungreased 8" square baking pan. Bake at 350 for 10-12 minutes. Meanwhile, beat eggs; add sugar, lemon juice and lemon zest; beat until thick and smooth (8-10 minutes). Sift together flour and baking powder; add to egg mixture and blend. Pour egg mixture gently over crust. Bake for 20-25 minutes. Cool slightly and sift powdered sugar over the top. Cool completely.

Notes:

If you want to double the recipe, use a 9x13" pan.

TEA TIME TREATS

SOUR CREAM PASTRIES

Preheat oven to 350 degrees

1 cup butter, cold
2 cups flour, sifted
1 egg yolk, beaten slightly
1/2 cup sour cream
1/2 cup apricot preserves
1/2 cup flaked coconut
1/4 cup chopped pecans
Granulated sugar

Cut butter into flour until it resembles fine crumbs (the more care you take with this step the better the pastry will be). Combine egg yolk and sour cream, blend into flour mixture. Form into a solid ball. Chill dough several hours or overnight. Divide dough into 4 equal parts; keep each part refrigerated until ready to use. Roll each part to 10" circle on lightly floured surface. Spread with 2 Tbsp. apricot preserves, sprinkle with 2 Tbsp. coconut and 1 Tbsp. nuts. Cut each circle into 8 wedges with pastry wheel or sharp knife. Starting with the wide end, roll each wedge into a crescent shape. Sprinkle with a little granulated sugar. Place on ungreased cookie sheet (I line mine with foil or parchment paper...less mess!) and bake at 350 degrees for 20 minutes. Remove from cookie sheet immediately and cool on rack.

Place the pointed tip underneath so crescent won't try to unroll. When rolling dough into a circle, roll from center to edge and give the dough a 1/4 turn after each roll.

TEA TIME TREATS

ORANGE LEMONADE

1-3/4 cups sugar or Splenda
2-1/2 cups water

2 Tbsp. grated lemon peel
2 Tbsp. grated orange peel
1-1/2 cups fresh lemon juice
1-1/2 cups fresh orange juice

In a large saucepan, combine sugar or Splenda and water. Cook over medium heat until sugar is dissolved, stirring occasionally.
Cool.

Add peel and juices to cooled sugar syrup. Cover and let stand at room temperature 1 hour. Strain syrup; cover and refrigerate.

To serve, fill glasses or pitcher with equal amounts of fruit syrup and water. Add ice and serve.

Makes about 12 servings

TEA TIME TREATS

CINNAMON ORNAMENTS

For years we used these mini ornaments made of cinnamon to tie, with a bit of raffia, onto our Cinnamon Sticks bags. People really enjoyed that special touch. These are nice for package ties or to hang on a tree at Christmas or Easter. They are nice all year long to hang in your car, bathroom or kitchen...a wonderful spicy fragrance. These are fun for kids to help make, too. They can be made with standard size cookie cutters or look for mini cutters at cookware stores. The larger ones can even be painted.

2 cups ground cinnamon
1-1/2 cups apple sauce

Make the dough a few days before you plan to cut it into shapes. It doesn't need to be refrigerated. Combine ground cinnamon and apple sauce until it is cookie dough consistency.

When ready to use, roll dough out on the shiny side of freezer paper. As you cut your shape, poke a hole for hanging in the top with a skewer. Allow finished ornaments to air dry for 3-4 days, turning occasionally, or place in oven on the lowest possible setting, again turning occasionally, until they are dry. Use a needle to thread ribbon or yarn through the hole; tie a knot, leaving a loop for hanging.

TEA TIME TREATS

NUT TASSIES

Preheat oven to 325 degrees.

1-1/2-2 cups nuts (pecans or walnuts)
2 eggs, slightly beaten
1-1/2 cups brown sugar, packed
2 Tbsp. butter, melted
1/2 tsp. vanilla
1/4 tsp. salt

Reserve 1/2 cup nuts, sprinkle remaining nuts into unbaked tart shells. Mix together remaining ingredients. Spoon into tart shells; sprinkle remaining nuts on top. Bake about 20 minutes. Cool 10 minutes, remove from pan. Cool completely on rack. Refrigerate leftover tarts. Makes about 3 dozen.

Tart Shells:
2 cups flour
1 cup butter, softened
2-3 ounces cream cheese, softened

Mix above ingredients; refrigerate for 30 min. Spray tart pans with Pam. Press rounded tsp. of pastry firmly and evenly into each tart cup.

TEA TIME TREATS

NOTES:

Instead of making the pastry yourself (although the cream cheese pastry is really good) you can purchase readymade pie crust (Pillsbury crusts work well) and cut rounds with a biscuit cutter or drinking glass. You can get about 17 rounds out of each pie crust by continuing to roll out leftover dough.

Be sure you have the mini tart pans for these tassies.

TEA TIME TREATS

CHRISTMAS MICE

In England, sugar mice are an old-fashioned tradition. Here is a fun chocolate version. They make great gifts. Arrange them on a cake plate for your holiday buffet table, put them on top of a cake for decoration, or use them as a surprise treat for a tea. Besides being cute they taste really good. Of course! They're chocolate!

About 60 maraschino cherries, with stems
Sliced almonds
1 (12 oz.) pkg. chocolate morsels
1 Tbsp. vegetable oil
About 60 chocolate kisses

Dry each cherry well with paper towel. Unwrap chocolate kisses. Melt chocolate morsels with the vegetable oil in the microwave. Holding a cherry by the stem, dip it into the chocolate, covering completely. Quickly stick a chocolate kiss onto the front for the head and insert sliced almonds between the cherry and the kiss for the ears. Place each finished mouse on a sheet of wax paper to dry. Makes about 60

TEA TIME TREATS

Notes:

TEA TIME TREATS

CINNAMON ROLLUPS

Preheat oven to 400 degrees

24 slices firm white sandwich bread, crusts trimmed
1 (8 oz.) pkg. cream cheese, softened
1 egg yolk (from large egg)
1-1/4 cup granulated sugar
1 Tbsp. ground cinnamon
1 stick unsalted butter, melted
1 cup nuts, chopped (optional)

Roll bread slices flat with a rolling pin. Mix cream cheese, egg yolk and 1/4 cup sugar. Spread a scant Tbsp. of mixture on each slice. Sprinkle with nuts, if desired. Roll up tightly.

Mix remaining sugar with the cinnamon in a shallow bowl. Brush rollups (including ends) with butter.
Roll in sugar mixture to coat. Place on cookie sheet; refrigerate or freeze at least 2 hours. (At this point you can place the rollups in an airtight freezer container and store for up to 2 months)

Bake rollups on cookie sheet 10 minutes until bottoms are glazed and brown.

Remove immediately to a wire rack to cool. Serve warm or cold; cut into pieces if desired.

Variation: you can substitute a flavored cream cheese, such as strawberry, omitting the cinnamon.

TEA TIME TREATS

Notes:

Last time I made these, I used the crustless Mrs. Bairds Iron Kids white bread and rolled it flat with a rolling pin. Works great!!

I find that adding the nuts makes these harder to roll and the nuts also tend to poke holes in the bread.

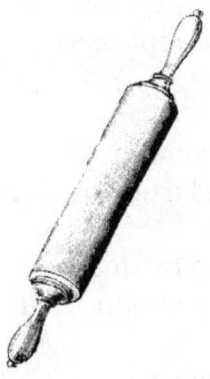

TEA TIME TREATS

STEAMED PLUM PUDDING WITH HARD SAUCE

1 cup flour

3 Tbsp. brown sugar, packed
1 tsp. cinnamon
1/2 tsp. baking powder
1/2 tsp. allspice
1/2 tsp. cloves
1/4 tsp. baking soda
1/2 cup milk
3 Tbsp. vegetable oil
2 Tbsp. molasses
1 egg

1 cup combined candied fruits or dried fruits
1/2 cup raisins
1/2 cup chopped nuts

Generously grease a 1-quart mold or casserole. Sift flour; place in medium bowl with all ingredients except mixed fruits, raisins and nuts. Mix until dry ingredients are moistened. Fold in fruits, raisins and nuts. Spoon into prepared mold. Cover with lid or foil. Place on wire rack in large steamer or kettle.

TEA TIME TREATS

Pour boiling water 3-4" deep into steamer; cover. Keep water boiling gently over low heat. If necessary, add more boiling water to maintain level. Steam for 1-1/2 to 2 hours or until pudding springs back when touched lightly in center. Cut into slices; serve warm with hard sauce. 6-8 servings

HARD SAUCE

2 cups powdered sugar, sifted
Pinch of salt
1/2 cup butter, softened
2 Tbsp. rum or brandy (or 2 tsp. rum or brandy extract)
1 tsp. vanilla

In small bowl, combine all ingredients. Beat at highest mixer speed until well blended. Chill until ready to serve. Makes 2 cups.

Notes:

This is a traditional English Christmas treat and not as hard as it sounds to make. I prefer dried fruits instead of candied fruits...things like dates, apricots, pears, etc. I have no idea why it's called "plum" pudding since I have yet to see a recipe for this that contains plums.

TEA TIME TREATS

BAKLAVA

Preheat oven to 325 degrees

4 cups (1 lb.) walnuts, finely chopped
1/2 cup sugar
1 tsp. ground cinnamon
1-1/4 cups butter, melted
1 (16 oz.) pkg. frozen phyllo dough, thawed
1-1/2 cups sugar
1/4 cup honey
1/2 tsp. lemon or grapefruit peel, finely grated
2 Tbsp. lemon or grapefruit juice, fresh squeezed
2 small (3") sticks of cinnamon

In a large mixing bowl, combine walnuts, ½ cup sugar and the ground cinnamon. Set aside.
Brush the bottom of 15x10x1 inch baking pan with some of the melted butter. Unfold phyllo dough. Layer about 1/4 of the phyllo sheets (approximately 8) in the pan, brushing each sheet generously with melted butter and allowing phyllo to extend up the sides of the pan. Sprinkle about 1-1/2 cups of the walnut filling over the top sheet. Repeat layers of phyllo and filling 2 more times.
Layer remaining phyllo sheets in the pan, brushing each sheet with butter. Drizzle any remaining butter over top layer. Trim edges of phyllo to fit pan. Using a sharp knife, cut through all layers to make triangles, diamonds or squares. Bake at 325 degrees for 45-50 minutes or until golden brown. Cool baklava slightly in its pan on a wire rack.

While baklava is baking in the oven, make the HONEY SAUCE: in a medium saucepan, stir together the 1 ½ cups

TEA TIME TREATS

sugar, honey, citrus peel and juice, stick cinnamon and 1 cup of water.

Bring to a boil. Reduce heat and simmer, uncovered, for 20 minutes. Remove sticks of cinnamon. Pour honey mixture over warm baklava. Cool completely before removing from pan. Makes about 50-60 pieces depending on how large you cut them.

Notes:

This is definitely easier with two people working together. Phyllo dough will dry out if left uncovered for long, so you need to lay all the sheets out on a clean tea towel and then cover them with plastic wrap. This is tricky but possible with one person. It is much easier if one person is carefully transferring each sheet to the pan while another person is doing the buttering of each sheet. Paul and I have gotten very good at working together on this recipe and we haven't had a disaster yet! We made baklava for many teas and other special occasions and we really prefer the grapefruit peel and juice.

BREADS&MUFFINS

BREADS & MUFFINS

Notes:

If you've never made yeast bread before...don't be afraid to try these recipes. If you follow the simple directions they are pretty much fool proof.

About 1-1/2 minutes on high in the microwave should give you the correct temperature for the water/butter mixture but check it with a thermometer to be sure.

I like to use bread flour but I've tried doing half bread flour and half whole wheat flour or half regular flour...it just depends on the texture you like. Experiment!

You can add all kind of goodies to your bread...dried cranberries, blueberries, cherries, apricots; sunflower seeds, pumpkin seeds, almonds, walnuts, etc. If adding dried fruits, use a combined amount of about 1/2 cup; if adding nuts or seeds, a combined amount of about 3/4 cup.

I make a cinnamon bread by adding about 3/4 cup chopped walnuts or pecans to the batter. When I've rolled out my dough rectangle I spread it with softened butter and sprinkle a mixture of 1/4 cup sugar and 1 Tbsp. Cinnamon over the butter. I roll the dough as tightly as I can so it won't separate between the layers.

BREADS&MUFFINS

BASIC BREAD

4 to 4-1/4 cups flour (I discuss types of flour in the notes)
 granulated sugar
2 Tbsp. non-fat dry milk
2 envelopes rapid rise yeast
2 tsp. salt
1-1/4 cups plus 2 Tbsp. Water
2 Tbsp. Butter (cut into pieces)

In a large bowl, combine 1 cup flour, sugar, dry milk, dry yeast and salt. Heat the water and butter together until very warm (120-130/). Gradually add the water/butter mixture to the dry ingredients and beat for 2 minutes at medium speed with an electric mixer scraping the sides of the bowl often. Add enough of the remaining flour to make a soft dough that can be worked by hand. If you are adding any fruit/nuts/?? to your bread, this is the time to stir them in. Put your dough mixture out onto a lightly floured board and knead for about 10 minutes. Continue to add a little flour to keep the dough from being sticky...it should be smooth and elastic. Cover with a clean tea towel and let it rest for 10 minutes. At the end of this first rise time; roll the dough out to a 12 x 8 rectangle. Starting from one short edge, rollup tightly. Pinch the bottom seam and the ends to seal. Place seam side down in a lightly greased 9 x 5 loaf pan. Cover and let rise in a warm place (I put mine in the microwave) for 45 minutes. Preheat the oven to 375 while the dough is rising. Bake for 35-40 minutes. Remove from pan immediately and cool on a wire rack.

BREADS&MUFFINS

REFRIGERATED BRAN MUFFINS

Preheat oven to 350 degrees

1/2 cup sugar
1/2 cup vegetable oil
2 eggs
2 cups buttermilk
2 -1/2 cups flour
2 -1/4 tsp. baking soda

1 cup boiling water
2-3 cups bran (I use Nabisco All Bran Cereal)
1 cup raisins or chopped dates

In a large bowl, pour boiling water over bran and dried fruit; blend and let sit to absorb moisture. In a medium bowl, blend together sugar, oil, eggs and buttermilk. Sift together flour and baking soda and add to the wet mixture. Stir in bran and fruit. Refrigerate batter overnight.

Fill greased muffin pans 2/3 full. Bake at 350 degrees for about 20 minutes.

NOTES: Unless you use a lot of buttermilk (does anyone???) it's difficult to keep around for the few times you need it. I use a powdered instant buttermilk mix; just add the powdered buttermilk in with the dry ingredients and add 2 cups of water to the sugar, oil and egg mixture.

This batter will keep in the refrigerator for up to 2 months. The baked muffins also freeze well. The muffins will come out better if the batter sets in the refrigerator overnight.

BREADS & MUFFINS

EASY DINNER ROLLS

1 envelope rapid rise yeast
2 Tbsp. sugar
1/2 cup milk
2 Tbsp. butter or margarine
2 cups bread flour
1 tsp. salt
1/4 cup water
1 small egg

Combine milk, water and butter and heat to 115-125 degrees. Place 1 cup flour, sugar, salt, egg and dry yeast in a large bowl. Add heated liquid and beat at medium speed on an electric mixer for 2 minutes. Slowly stir in remaining 1 cup of flour. On a lightly floured board, knead the dough until smooth and elastic, about 10 minutes.

Cover and let rest for 10 minutes. Divide dough into two equal parts. Roll each part out and cut into 12 equal parts. Roll each small piece of dough into a ball. Lightly grease or spray 12 muffin cups (3" size). Place 2 pieces of dough into each muffin cup. Preheat the oven to 400 degrees. Cover and let dough rise in a warm place for about 30 minutes. Bake 10-15 minutes or until browned. Remove from pans and serve warm or cool. Makes 12 rolls.

BREADS&MUFFINS

Notes:

BREADS & MUFFINS

SPOON BREAD

Preheat oven to 350 degrees

4-7 jalapeno peppers, seeded and chopped
2 eggs
1 cup cream corn
1 small onion, chopped
1 (2 oz.) can black olives, sliced
2 Tbsp. vegetable oil
1 tsp. garlic powder
1 tsp. baking powder
1/2 tsp. ground cumin
3/4 cup cornmeal
2 cups cheddar cheese, shredded and divided

In a medium mixing bowl, beat eggs. Add corn, onion, olives, oil and chopped jalapenos. Combine garlic powder, baking powder, cumin and corn meal. Add to egg mixture with 1 cup of the cheese; stir until blended. Grease 9" square pan; pour mixture into pan and sprinkle remaining 1 cup of shredded cheese over the top. Bake at 350 degrees for 35-40 minutes.

Notes:

If you don't like spicy food you can cut back to 1 or 2 Jalapeno peppers or leave them out completely.

Try adding about 1/2 cup of bacon to this recipe; fried until crisp and then crumbled.

BREADS & MUFFINS

MORNING GLORY MUFFINS

Preheat oven to 350 degrees

2 cups all-purpose flour
1-1/4 cups white sugar
2 tsp. baking soda
2 tsp. ground cinnamon
1/4 tsp. salt

2 cups carrots, shredded
1/2 cup dried cherries, roughly chopped
1/2 cup walnuts, lightly toasted and chopped
1/2 cup coconut, unsweetened, flaked (optional)
1 apple, cored and shredded

3 eggs
1 cup vegetable oil
2 tsp. vanilla extract

Grease 12 muffin cups. In a large bowl, mix together the flour, sugar, soda, cinnamon and salt with a wire whisk. Stir in the carrots, cherries, walnuts, coconut (if desired) and apple.

In a separate bowl, beat together eggs, oil and vanilla. Stir egg mixture into the dry mix until just moistened. Distribute evenly in the muffin cups. Bake for 20 minutes or until a toothpick inserted into the center of a muffin comes out clean.

These are the yummiest muffins I've ever made!!

BREADS&MUFFINS

BLUEBERRY STREUSEL MUFFINS

Preheat oven to 375 degrees

1/4 cup butter, softened
1/3 cup sugar
1 egg
1 tsp. vanilla extract
2-1/3 cups all-purpose flour
4 tsp. baking powder
1/2 tsp. salt
1 cup milk
1-1/2 cups fresh or frozen blueberries

Streusel topping:
1/2 cup sugar
1/3 cup all-purpose flour
1/2 tsp. ground cinnamon
1/4 cup cold butter

In a large bowl, cream butter and sugar. Beat in egg and vanilla; mix well. Combine the flour, baking powder and salt; add to creamed mixture alternately with milk. Fold in blueberries carefully.

Fill 12 greased muffin cups two-thirds full. In a small bowl, combine the sugar, flour, and cinnamon. Cut in butter until crumbly. Sprinkle over muffins.

Bake for 25-30 minutes or until browned. Cool for 5 minutes before removing to a wire rack. Serve warm. Store leftovers lightly covered to keep streusel topping from getting soft.

BREADS&MUFFINS

BANANA NUT BREAD

When I have some bananas I've let get too ripe to eat I make a loaf of this bread...the riper the bananas are, the better they are for baking because of the increased sugar content. We like this bread for breakfast; toast it in a little butter or serve cold, it's good either way. It's also good spread with cream cheese for tea sandwiches.

Preheat oven to 350 degrees

1/2 cup vegetable oil
3/4 cup sugar
2 eggs, beaten
3 bananas, mashed (VERY RIPE)
2 cups flour
1 tsp. baking soda
1/2 tsp. baking powder
1/2 tsp. salt
3 Tbsp. milk
1/2 tsp. vanilla extract
1/2 cup nuts, chopped (optional)

Beat oil and sugar together. Add eggs and banana pulp and beat well. Add sifted dry ingredients, milk, and vanilla. Mix well; stir in nuts (if using). Pour into greased 9x5 loaf pan and bake at 350 degrees for 45-55 minutes. Check for doneness after 45 minutes by inserting a tester into the center...if it comes out clean, the bread is done. After about 10 minutes, remove loaf from pan and cool completely on wire rack. Wrap in foil and store overnight before cutting.

BREADS&MUFFINS

Makes 4 small loaves or 2 large loaves. It will make 7 of the "baby" loaves which are wonderful for gifts. The baby loaves will take less baking time; check after about 30 minutes. Loaves are done when a tester comes out clean. This recipe makes 8 mini loaves if you want to use it for gifts. Bake for 25-30 minutes.

BREADS & MUFFINS

ZUCCHINI-WALNUT BREAD

Preheat oven to 350 degrees

3/4 cup whole-wheat flour
3/4 cup all-purpose flour
1 tsp. baking powder
1/4 tsp. baking soda
1/4 tsp. salt
1 tsp. ground cinnamon
1/4 tsp. ground nutmeg

2 large egg whites at room temperature
1 cup sugar (or 1/2 cup Splenda)
1/2 cup unsweetened applesauce
2 Tbsp. canola oil
1/4 tsp lemon extract
1 cup zucchini, grated, lightly packed
1 Tbsp. walnuts, toasted and chopped

Coat 2-6" x 3" loaf pans with cooking spray. Whisk dry ingredients together in a large bowl. Whisk egg whites, sugar or Splenda, applesauce, oil and lemon extract in a medium bowl. Stir in zucchini.
Make a well in the center of the dry ingredients; slowly mix in the zucchini mixture with a rubber spatula. Fold in the walnuts. Do not over mix. Transfer the batter to the two prepared loaf pans.
Bake the loaves until a toothpick comes out almost clean, about 40-45 minutes. Cool in the pan on a wire rack for about 5 minutes, then turn out onto the rack to cool completely.

BREADS & MUFFINS

BLUEBERRY OATMEAL MUFFINS (OR PEACH OR APPLE)

Preheat oven to 400 degrees

1-1/4 cups all-purpose flour
1 cup quick-cooking oats
1/2 cup packed brown sugar
2 tsp. baking powder
1/2 tsp. salt
1/2 tsp. ground cinnamon
1/4 tsp. ground nutmeg
3/4 tsp. baking soda

1 egg, lightly beaten
1 cup (8 oz.) plain yogurt
1/4 cup butter, melted
1 cup fresh blueberries (substitute fresh peaches, cut into bite-size chunks, or shredded apple to make 1 cup)

In a large bowl, combine the first eight ingredients. Combine the egg, yogurt and butter; stir into the dry ingredients just until moistened. Fold in fruit.

Coat muffin cups with cooking spray. Divide mixture evenly into 12 muffin cups. Bake for 18-22 minutes or until a toothpick inserted in the middle of one of the muffins comes out clean. Cool for 5 minutes before removing from pan to a wire rack. Serve warm.

Makes 12 muffins

BREADS & MUFFINS

PUMPKIN BREAD

Preheat oven to 350 degrees

3 -1/2 cups flour
2 cups granulated sugar
2 tsp. baking soda
1 tsp. ground cinnamon
1 tsp. ground nutmeg
1 tsp. salt
2 cups pumpkin (canned and not pie mix)
4 eggs
1 cup vegetable oil
3/4 cup water
1/2 cup nuts, chopped (optional)

In large mixing bowl, sift together dry ingredients. Make a well in the center and add pumpkin, eggs, oil and water; mix until smooth. Add nuts (if using). Pour into greased 9 9x5 loaf pans, filling 1/2 full (makes 2 loaves). Bake at 350 degrees for 50-60 minutes. Take loaves out of pans after about 10 minutes; cool completely on rack.

The recipe will make about 15 mini loaves for gift giving. Bake for about 25-30 minutes.

The authors

Paul is an Electrical Engineer and Peggy is a musician, teacher and writer. They both enjoy new experiences, an attitude which led them to get involved in helping start Cinnamon Sticks in 1984. In 1989, they decided to open a Tea Room inside Cinnamon Sticks. Despite the fact that neither of them had any food service experience, they successfully operated Cinnamon Sticks Tea Room until 2003 when they decided to sell the business. Since then, both Paul and Peggy have been involved in many projects and have devoted time to family and friends. While they worked daily in the tea room and shop, they had no time to produce a much requested cookbook. After selling the business, they wrote and published their cookbook. Many new recipes have been added since the first edition was published in 2005.

www.ingramcontent.com/pod-product-compliance
Lightning Source LLC
Chambersburg PA
CBHW051751040426
42446CB00007B/310